MY
HOLY SPIRIT

Seven Steps, Seven Ways

ROBERT SCHOFIELD

outskirts
press

ACKNOWLEDGMENTS

I would like to thank God for the Blessing of the Holy Spirit. He has blessed me with a light that can only come from the Holy Spirit to lead me in the Gospel of Grace. As He has done with Peter, I feel He has done with me, giving me solid ground to build my Faith in Christ Jesus who has promised the Holy Spirit of God to us all; if we ask for Him. I believe He is real and the third person of the Holy Trinity.

I am always thankful to my fellow Ministers and Pastors for their continued advice and helpful verses of the Bible to lead me on a path of righteous words of understanding.

A debt of deepest and loving gratitude is to be given to my Wife Gloria for 62 understanding years. Her encouragement and protection of me against all and many odds that have tried to put my light's out. She has served me to increase my spiritual beliefs, grammar, spelling attributes and the awesome pictures and drawings displayed here.

There is a very special Woman that I need to thank; if it wasn't for her I probably would not have put this Seven Steps Seven Ways, into book form! Ms Authire Leach guided me in the right direction each and every day we meet for consultation. Thank you Ms Authire I'm so glad that I meet you before you went on to be with our Lord in heaven!

A blessed thank you to all those who attended the Power for Living Classes on Sunday mornings, they were a lot more interesting because of your participation.

A special thanks to Pastor Ralph Sims, and to his loving wife Minister Monica for all their support.

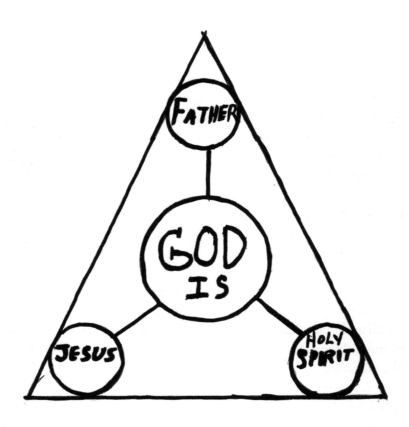

TABLE OF CONTENTS

My Understanding of the Holy Spirit

THE HOLY SPIRIT is in the world today! He is the third person of the Holy Trinity. He is the most earnest servant that God could hope for. He was there in the beginning with God the Father and the Son! In (Genesis-2) He is the Spirit sent to hover over the waters of the Earth. He did as Almighty God commanded Him i.e. "remove a portion of the waters to the firmament of the air" which God called the Sky. I love these next two bible quotes, both have ten words one is the first ten words of the bible and the other is almost the last ten words of the bible. (Genesis-1) "In the beginning God created the Heavens and the Earth". (Revelation 21-1) "I saw a new Heaven descend on a new Earth." In the first one the Holy Spirit was working with the commands of God, and the 2nd the Apostle John was in the Spirit when he saw the vision of God's Heaven descending on a new earth. I believe these are some of the most beautiful ten word quotes that can excite us all. The very last ten words come from Jesus (Revelations 22-21, "The Grace of the Lord Jesus is with Gods people."

God is a Triune God and most Christians would confess to this. He is not three separate persons but three persons in one God the Father, the Son/

Jesus and the Holy Spirit/Holy Ghost. Science has caused us to look at things from their view, I as a creationist, look to the Bio/Genesis theory of the (5) Five Laws I.E. As found in Genesis 1-1 relating to TIME- FORCE- ACTION- SPACE-AND, MATTER): The first ten words of the Bible show us this; **Time -** In the beginning, **Force-** God, **Action-** created, **Space** the Heavens -**Matter** Earth.(Genesis 1-1)"In the beginning God created the heavens and the earth".

The fact of the matter is that we can see that all three members of the Holy Trinity have been around even before the beginning of time as we know it?

God, whom no one except for Jesus and the Holy Spirit has seen, has said in (Genesis 1-26) "let **US** make man in **OUR** image in **OUR** likeness". God is more than one person but only one God; He is the Godhead of the Holy Trinity, the Father, the Son and the Holy Spirit! (JOHN 1:1-2) "That which was in the beginning was the word, and the word was with God and the word was God, He was with God in the beginning"! This verse from John is associated with Jesus; I offer this, God is the Father and the Son and the Holy Spirit, then the Holy Spirit possesses Divine attributes that are found in each of the God Heads! I can see seven of them;

1. Omniscience, that He is all knowing. (1 Corinthian 6-11)
2 Omnipresence, He is always present. (Ps 139-7)
3. Omnipotence, He is the Almighty. (Gen 1-2)
4. Truth, He is all things that are or have been stated to be true. (John 5-6)
5. Holiness, He is the pure quality of all things. (Luke 11-13)
6. As life, He is the beginning and end of all life. (Rom 8-2)
7. Wisdom, He is the accumulated knowledge of all things. (Isa 40-13).

The Deity of the Spirit is proven by His being equally associated with the other persons of the Holy Trinity.
(Acts 1-8, Matt 28-19; and (2 Corinthian: 13-14)

MY FOREWORD
ON THE HOLY SPIRIT

WHAT WAS I thinking? Why a book on the Holy Spirit! There are many books written on the Holy Spirit. The Holy Spirit was given to many people in the Bible. I hope to use stories of them as an example of the visions and meaning of each of the Seven Steps. For instance, Job is my favorite example of being led by the Holy Spirit of God! No man of Faith has had to endure more pain, sorrow, and loss of life and property, he at all times, while in the Spirit, even like Satan tempted Eve and Eve tempted Adam; Job also was tempted by Satan and Job's wife to walk away from God but he remained faithful to God the Father Almighty! I realized that Gods Holy Spirit was calling on me to be one with Him; the only way was, (I felt at the time) was to be Baptized in or with the Holy Spirit I remember a quote by Billy Graham saying that the Holy Spirit is God; as outlined in the Bible. Baptism of the Holy Spirit is not like with the Water Baptism for cleansing and rising up from the water for a new life in Christ Jesus; but it is the bestowal of a Spiritual Gift, to be empowered for a Christian Ministry. I know that there are different doctrines and concepts of theology that separate the denominations of religion; and that their separation is not very far away from each other.

The concept of Salvation is all the same as far as I can see! (John 14-6 Paraphrased) you see we all need to perfect our Christian walk and beliefs to accept Christ Jesus as our Lord and Savior in order to gain entrance into Heaven! Therefore we need to perfect our way of life on this earthly journey; for we pass this way but once in our life time and we need to get it right; and that is to be empowered with the Holy Spirit of God to move forward and comply with the teaching of Christ Jesus! So why write about the Holy Spirit? There must be thousands of Books on the Holy Spirit? My choice of the terminology of Seven Steps Seven Ways outlines a practical view thru stories for those who may be stuck in a Biblical description, of Bible history? A simple view is a way I hope to bring out for all to be able to see the Holy Spirit more clearly. (7 Steps 7 Ways equals 49 reasons)

I WOULD OFFER THIS PRAYER

As in the opening of any Church service or Bible class we need to start with a Prayer.

May my Prayer oh Lord be a Positive and Powerful one to your liking! Oh heavenly Father; in what way can we serve the Church? Let us see the truth in serving you. Father God let your ears hear all who gather in your name today. We seek your truth through your holy word that is found in the Gospel of truth. We look for the words how the Holy Spirit will explain the uses of the elements of the earth to create in us a foundation that gives life to all things on earth. Oh Lord let not your words sit still in the bindings of a book. Let all who Evangelize, Prophesies, Preach or Teach of your Holy word do it with great Joy and Understanding.

The words of knowledge and wisdom you give to us brings together all those who seek your face. Send your Holy Spirit to all those who approach your Altar to proclaim your Son Jesus in the Sacrament of Holy Communion. Oh Father God let your Grace, Mercies and Peace be in our hearts; my Lord my God, melt me, mold me, make of me, use me, as I offer myself to abide in you forever more. In name of Jesus the Son of God Amen.

THE SERVANT OF GOD

THE FIRST OF SEVEN STEPS

Chapter 1

———— ～～ ————

As a Servant of God

IN THE CREATION of the heavens and the earth, when God spoke to have all things created, the Holy Spirit obeyed and performed as a loving servant of God Almighty! (Gen 1)

The word of God tells us, the earth was without form and He had the Holy Spirit hover over the earth and removes a portion of the water to the firmament above the earth and God called it the sky. I believe this very same amount of water was used to flood the earth during the time of Noah. This water is replaced every time it rains the sun then cause's evaporation in order to send it back into the sky above.

When I envision what the Holy Spirit did in the creation, it was all about preparing the earth for the coming of mankind. The Spirit removed the water and sent it to the sky above thus exposing the land and the *mountainous* areas. Thus the water that collected on the tops of the mountains would freeze up and will be released when the sunshine hits them. Then the melted ice would form into water and cause streams and rivers to form. This water would then go to feed mankind and the great forest that would produce oxygen for mankind to breath. The streams and rivers would continue to the great pastures and valleys of the earth so that mankind could grow crops for their sustenance. God spoke let there be light and the sun replaced the darkness. He spoke again so that a moon would appear when the sun would set thus causing alight during the dark times.

God spoke that the Spirit would form all life in the waters and on the earth and those things of the air would be formed.

The Holy Spirit performed as the great servant of God, in the creation of the earth and all living things to include mankind.

In the (7) seven chapters to be discussed, each one is considered by me to be a step that the Holy Spirit has taken to lead us. There will be (49) forty nine different ways to present the understanding of the Holy Spirit.

I would like to go back in time, to the book of Acts (Acts 2-2) and the day of Pentecost when Peter referred to the book of (Joel 2-28). Saint Peter was explaining about what had just occurred with the flames of fire lighting on the heads of each one in the room as a time in the future. i.e.: In Joel God said, "I will pour out my Spirit on all people and all flesh." and Joel talked about the last days. Peter said to the people who were new Christians, how God made it possible for all of them to receive the Holy Spirit, and this was done on the first day of the Church's beginning! This is the beginning of a new era that the work of Jesus was completed and it would be continued by the Holy Spirit. The book of Acts tells us, it would first be for the Apostles, and their Disciples.

Then all of the world would receive Him, as long as they accept Christ first as their Savior.

How did you and I receive the Holy Spirit? God gave all those present the Holy Spirit on the Day of Pentecost. It was God who gave the Spirit before that day. God decided who was to receive Him. The day after the Pentecost a new born again Christian would need to ask of God for the Holy Spirit to come into their lives as they were being Baptized. On that first day the whole Church was given the Holy Spirit for dispensation, and now it's not a question of Gods willingness to give the Spirit; but of the Christians willingness to receive Him. Each of us must want to accept Him and be willing to be led by Him all the days of our lives!

a.   We will not be able to See Him as we look, at each other, but we should be able to see Him in our minds and our hearts. God said that He would write everything we need to know on our hearts. The Holy Spirit will then make visual to us what is needed and by that He makes it possible for us to see Him as we use the needs of our hearts!

b.   Surely we will be able to hear just like the thunder of a storm He comes to us we just have to pay attention and listen to what He has to say to our minds and our hearts!

c.   Giving this is more than pledges, tithes, or donations. We can give back in many ways, but the Spirit gives to us the incentive to do more by through our use of the talents that God has given to us. He gives us an insight on each and everything we will ever do. In Luke 12-15 tells us, "One's life does not consist in the abundance of his possessions". The Holy Spirit will be right there for us insuring us we will be able to reach all our goals so long as we ask for His help.

d.   When we put all of the ways of this servant of God to mind, we will be guided in all we do. The Spirit is our counselor with that He is able to assist us in all matters of the heart and the mind. He is the one that will set us straight and correct us in all we do. We all get urges do things not of good standing, but the Spirit will give us the urges we need to stay on the right path. (Ask for His help)

e.   What does it really mean to share with others? Jesus said "Love one another"; this was given as a command in John 15-17. Without love we cannot share! God told us of a special invitation in Psalm 139-14: "We praise you oh Lord God almighty because we are fearfully made". We are made in His image, He is love and He shares it with us, so let us share it with one another! We can find joy in our salvation and in sharing what God has given to each of us.

f.   How can we be helping those who are in need? Luke 11-19, says "I tell you, ask and it will be given to you; seek and you will find; knock and it will be opened to you. Your friend knocks on your door after midnight; he is there to ask of you something; it must be important otherwise he would not come at this time of day! The Spirit encourages us to help one another so let us be diligent, for we pass this way but once in life, let us do well to one another.

g.   The Holy Spirit is our connection to Jesus, his intercession is to pose, frame and reword anything we have to say, so that when presented to God we are not mumbling. When we ask, pray, or look for the things in our hearts, He makes the words true and clear for God to hear them.

The Seven Ways of the Servant of God:

1

ALL SEEING

a.   Seeing (1 Corinthians 2-10-15) God has revealed himself to us thru the Holy Spirit! The Dove is seen in Mathew 3-16 as a vision of the Spirit that came upon Jesus during His baptism. The Spirit sees into our hearts and reads those things we need to know in our path in life. He reveals to us those deep thoughts within us that God has planted there. Man has a spirit within himself and the Holy Spirit talks to that spirit of man. No-one knows the thoughts of God except the Spirit of God. It's not like the spirit of the world; those things are not of God. We tend to see the world for fun, games, desires, habits and what others perceive as needs for a life within Gods ways? We must remember that the world is weak and thinks things of the flesh rather that of the word of God! We are not able to see the Spirit physically; however He is with us always. In 1-Corinthians 5-6 Yeast is used as a symbol of impurity, when you sprinkle the yeast over the dough and you knead it, to work it all the way thru the dough so that it will rise. This is the way of sin as it works its way in your life. We need to live as the Spirit will lead us, as we call upon him for his desires! We get to use our Spirit as yeast and use the Holy Spirit to melt in us and mold us to a Godly perfection.

Do you remember the song "Mine eyes have seen the glory of the coming of the Lord?" He enables us to have that vision of the power of God thru His actions.

The following verses remind me of the story of Peter and John evangelizing in Jerusalem and being arrested by the Sanhedrin!

Psalm 51:4-9, they were able to, "see beyond any evil thing man could do in the sight of the Lord," what they did most likely is; you and I can do by asking for the Spirit to, "create in me a new heart O'God and renew a steadfast Spirit with-in me."

With the Holy Spirit in us we can like the Apostles be full of the Spirit of God in all matters! Peter and John were arrested for evangelizing and performing miracles, and this drew the attention of the Sanhedrin's, who were afraid they might lose power over the people? They were willing to let the Apostles go if they promised not to preach in Jerusalem again! The Apostles told them, that would not work because; "who should they obey God or you?" The people saw all they did thru the power of the Holy Spirit. One of the miracle's I see here is the Sanhedrin wanted them to stop preaching but they did not forbid the evangelizing of the resurrection of Jesus the Christ.

The Apostles prayed a prayer of thanksgiving; one not of deliverance but that of not to be oppressed but to be made freer to perform with extra boldness in their evangelizing! Verse (31) they prayed at the place they had their meetings; the room was shaken up and they were all filled with the renewing of the Holy Spirit, they were able to continue to speak the word of God boldly?

We use the Holy Spirit to seek the path we need to follow, by doing this we are able to see what is written on our hearts and follow the path thru the Holy Spirits leading.

God has chosen each of us as He has the Apostles, (John 15:16) He has also given to us the Holy Spirit so that we might see His works in us for the very purpose, as a deposit of safety that will guarantee us protection to go forth and preach His Holy Word without fear!

(2 Corinthians 5:7) "We live by Faith and not by sight." Jesus

promised us the Holy Spirit would come to all who asked for Him and believed that Jesus is the Son of God and that thru Him all things are possible! The Spirit sees our path in life and He is here to guide us along life's path way, and to convict us of the truth, and comfort us in all matters of our lives! If the birth of Jesus thru the Holy Spirit had not happened we would not have the insight we need to see the world thru the eyes of the Holy Spirit of God.

Back in the first century they did not see the word of God as we see it today, manifested in the pages of our bibles. They heard the word thru Disciples of Jesus and the Spirit gave them the words to say from their inner hearts. A blind person in fact could conceive the Holy Word easier than one who could see! There are thousands of Braille workers around the world helping the Blind and the vision impaired touch the promises of Christ. They are using hearing devices to receive the words of the Bible. These persons are all inspired by the Holy Spirit to assist those in need of hearing aids and printed on special embossed paper to give them a special vision of the works of the New Testament.

The story of Saul to Paul; also fits the all Seeing of the Holy Spirit. You see Paul acclaimed that Jesus did appear to him that day on the road to Damascus he had with him warrants to arrest members of the Jesus movement or the Way people and Disciples of Jesus; in-order to put them in prison for persecution. The book of Acts can be called the Acts of the Holy Spirit as so many were given the Holy Spirit in the accounting of this Book! Paraphrased (Acts 9:1-19) A loud noise like thunder then a flashing of light appeared and all those around saw this as they were traveling on the road to Damascus with Saul; Saul was in the middle of the light but no one could see him, or hear the conversation between him and our Lord Jesus. Jesus called to him saying "Saul, Saul, why have you persecuted me." Saul answered who are you Lord? Jesus whom you persecuted; Jesus gave him directions to go and wait for a man named Ananias. As Saul got up he realized he was blind the men with him had to lead him. A man Ananias was given a dream to go to Saul and lay hands on him to give him back his sight. Ananias was not happy because he knew that Saul was a murder of Jesus's followers. But he did as the Lord asked. He laid hands on him and he could see again;

he also baptized him. Saul may have received the Holy Spirit at the same time. That's why he declared that he was an Apostle of Christ Jesus. He Saul then disappeared for several years preaching most likely in Arabia!

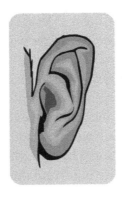

2

HEARING

b. Hearing (Acts 19-2) When Paul was traveling thru the city of Ephesus, he meet with some people and asked them if they received the Holy Spirit, when they first believed? What is the Holy Spirit they asked back? We received the baptism of John for repentance! They must have shown they were strong in their belief, because Paul upon hearing this baptized them immediately into the Holy Spirit These disciples heard the word of the repentance, but not the connection of the spirit within them and the one of God. Christ was made known to them; they believed and testified to their new Faith Jesus Christ!

When John was in the Spirit in the book of Revelation, a message was given to all Seven Church's. The Spirit gave them each a message as to how they were conducting themselves! The Spirit said to each of them at the end of His message to them, "To he who has an ear, let him hear what the Spirit says to the Church's". Each Church was told if they were to overcome those things that were wrong in their Church they would be able to eat from the Tree of Life in paradise, or would not be hurt by the second death, one could receive a new white stone with a new name on it known only to them.

Ask yourself this question? How do we recognize the Holy Spirit of God? This is the very same Spirit that is within you, that Jesus asked God to send to us when He left to be at the right hand of God! 1 John 4:2, "this is how you can recognize the Spirit of God; every spirit, (like you and I were born with) that acknowledges Jesus the Christ that has come in the flesh is from God." We are all born with a spirit that comes from God and this is how we are able to hear and see the Holy Spirit of God that is within us! We are not able to hear Him until we accept Jesus as the Son of God!

We are God's temple are we not? God is love and we can't love unless with live our lives in love-we are then able to love Him because, "He first loved us." (1 John 4:19).

1 Corinthians 12:12; Paul talks about the body being made up of many parts! Some parts being more gifted than others but all are very important in-order for the whole body to function. Our hands are not connected to our feet; each one is designed to perform different move-ments as is the eyes and the ears they too perform separate but much needed functions. The thing is that all of our body parts must get along with each other. The Holy Spirit dwelling within us insures that there is a unity of each functioning part.

We are the Temple of God, thus we are all a part of the body of Christ? Each of us therefore has different gifts and talents to enable the church to function. Some of the gifts and talents are geared to working for the Church as a gardener, custodian, even singing in the choir: Some are even blessed to hear the effects of the music and songs that are sung.

Our eyes cannot hear or speak for us. Whenever we hear sounds our Head turns with the direction of our eyes that look to where the sounds are coming from. Whenever God speaks to us or Jesus, even the Holy Spirit I personally close my eyes; and listen with my heart because the Holy Spirit moves us to hear what we need to hear. Remember this; it will not be like the thunder of a storm but close, close enough that we should feel the quake of the mind, to even our hearts wanting. Our body parts have a mutual understanding of each other; just like the congregation of a Church. Each person in the church uses the gifts and the talents God has given them in-order for the church to function as one body in Christ!

3

GIVING

c.   Giving (2 Corinthians 1:22). The word of God as given to us by Christ the anointed assures we have a deposit of security in that, God will fulfill each and all of His promises! Jesus said in (John 14:14) "you may ask me anything in my name and I will give it". Giving is the ultimate reward from the Holy Spirit, all we have to do is ask and he will give it. The Holy Spirit insures us our needs will be fulfilled each and every time we go to Him. As long as He indwells within us you can be sure He is looking after our comfort. Jesus said in John 14:16; "I will ask the Father and He will give you another counselor to be with you forever".

The Holy Spirit gives us help, comfort, ideas, strength, encouragement and will intercede for us with God on any mater. You don't have to know what to say or how to pray, He will make the interpretation for you and give it to God as it should be in the name of Christ Jesus!

Jesus has taught us that the Holy Spirit will indwell in us, and will help us remember things that were written on our hearts by God. The Holy Spirit will give to us a teaching of righteousness and judgment and lead all believers to the truth.

The world is against the Holy Spirit, they say when Christ left the world the void was never filled, this is because they cannot see Him nor do they believe in Him.

Where shall we find grace to go the way Jesus went, especially as he did in the wilderness with the Holy Spirit within Him. Jesus met and overcame the Tempter. Jesus definitely had obeyed the Fathers voice that He heard according to scriptures teaching us that death has no authority over Him or any of us for we shall find grace to go the same way as the First church of God went showing obedience to the Holy Spirit. We should all be willing to learn what the Spirit is teaching and giving to us!

The Holy Spirit is not an impersonal force like a cloud or gravity.

He is as much of a person as God the Father and Christ the Son; they are all persons and each has a personal nature about them! We are not to refer to God, Jesus or the Holy Spirit as an (it); they are a (He), and we should not grieve them at all!

All gifts come from heaven and the Holy Spirit usually is the one who delivers all the gifts. The Holy Spirit is known for providing us with the Gifts of the Spirit. The gift of Love is needed to exercise our talents and abilities that He has given to us that are written on our hearts.

In Titus 3:5, "He saved us not because we were good enough or by any deeds we did; but because of His kindness and pity, and the washing away of our sins. He also gave to us the indwelling of His Holy Spirit."

Once we are saved thru Christ our Lord, we should feel a compelling urge to do good works and good deeds. For this is the very nature of Christ thru the Holy Spirit of God!

In Chapter 7, the benefits of seeing the Holy Spirit are with-in our spiritual being: where God has placed Him to give us hindsight so that we can share our abilities. This is a different Giving than this Giving as the Holy Spirit is giving us what we need to be a part of a ministry to share with others. In both cases of Giving we are using our teaching from the Word of God through and from the Holy Spirit.

4

CORRECTING

d.   Correcting (2 Corinthians 3-6-5-6) Wow I wish I hadn't said that, or I'm too confused to speak? Some gifted people never learn to use their gifts of speech or to think in the right way? Certain people focus on the genius of their own creativity, not realizing that they just need to keep it simple. The Holy Spirit will correct and send the message you are trying to relay to God the Father. The Holy Spirit is going to correct whatever you say; when He passes on your supplications to the Father it will be just what the Father needs to hear, in order to respond to you

You can call upon the Holy Spirit any time you need Him, it will be thru your Faith that your heart will open up to Him? Your mind will hear his voice and you must believe and trust, He will correct and give you guidance to whatever you ask of Him!

You may even talk to God anytime, you can pray to Him, ask specific question of Him, or you can share with Him your experiences of yesterday or today. In whatever you do with talking to God thru the Holy Spirit, be patient in waiting for an answer. Remember this your time is not the same time God works by?

We should all be reminded that the God Head is at work for you thru the Holy Spirit; the power to correct any situation or comply with any request comes from God. God is three persons in one God, the Father is in Jesus and Jesus is in the Spirit Jesus is in the Father, they are in each other but they are not each other! God is all three persons and with that kind of power on your side He can correct any problem or situation that can arise. You have a Spirit that is within you that God put there at birth, and it yearns to talk openly with the Holy Spirit. Jesus said "ask and you will receive; seek and you will find it; knock and a door will be opened to you".

Paul also talked about all the problems of life that we are faced with; like hardships, these can be corrected by you trusting the Holy Spirit will interpret them from where God wrote on the Tablets of your heart. Those things written their by God the Father; God has made it easy for us to correct any thing we say or do, once again the Holy Spirit is to give you the answer, as He interprets what is needed!

The Holy Spirit causes us to remember things that Jesus taught us; for instance in Romans 5:6, "You see, at the right time, when we were still powerless, Christ died for our sins." I remember a friend of mine told me she didn't want to think about religion anymore. This statement is coming from a Pastors kid that gave up simply because she got tired of hearing this phrase, "I, a poor miserable sinner," these words were from a Lutheran confessional hymnal. She further stated that she was feed up with being told how bad she was. You know she should have remembered the rest of the verse; it went on like this, Jesus tells us that "God forgives us-poor, miserable sinners," that we are! The Holy Spirit is ready to correct us and this reminds us that Jesus gave His life for people such as us, sinners! Wow my friend missed the point of being saved having come from death to life in Jesus the Christ our Lord. We have all gone from poor, miserable sinners to abundantly blessed, joyful saints. Call upon the Spirit to help you correctly seek out your needs!

Remember this we have become righteous in Gods' eye, because His Son died on the cross for all our sins; and we believed that He Jesus is the Son of God.

Mark 10: 13-16 Do you remember the little children and Jesus? The people were bringing the little children to Him, but the Disciples were rebuking them to stop; Jesus said, "Let the little children come to me, and do not hinder them, for the kingdom of God belongs to such as these. Jesus corrected the Disciples, he was making a point that we too need to be like little children in or learning or we may not enter into God's kingdom of Heaven.

5

SHARING

e.   Sharing (2 Peter 1-21:2 Corinthians 5-5). The characteristics of man, is of a sinful nature, man must call upon the Holy Spirit to lead him in a life of spiritual righteousness. Why is the Holy Spirit so important in the life of a Christian? Many people and Christians alike have said the Holy Spirit is something of the past. It was for the early Church and He has left us. In the book of Acts we see a clear picture that he was there for the Disciples and all who were present at the time. He came to us as a Flame of Fire, lighting on each person! There were thousands of early Jewish believers and many more Gentiles! We can receive the Holy Spirit during our Baptism; all we have to do is ask God for him at that time? All believers have a Spirit indwelling them, but all do not ask for the Holy Spirit to fill their hearts with what he can share with our spirit within us.

Being filled with the Holy Spirit does produce a sense of the Fruits of the Spirit I.e. Love, Joy, Peace, Goodness, Gentleness, Patience, Kindness, Faithfulness and Self-control. These we shall share with one-another. In (Romans 8-6) "the mind of a sinful man is death, but the mind shared by the Spirit is life and peace." Which would you rather have, Life or Death? You can receive one of the two kinds of spiritual states; Death is forever and it's a Spirit filled world of pain and anguish forever in Hell. The other is a spiritual filled life to be led here on Earth and then one in the Spiritual Heaven. This too is promised by Jesus to live an eternal life because of Gods salvation. The Holy Spirit brings one not into a form of anxious bondage, but it will unite us as one in Christ; enabling one to share his Son-ship!

There is a most eloquent passage in (Romans 8: 31-35) it speaks about who would dare to oppose believers; that are filled with the Holy Spirit, when absolutely nothing can separate Christians from Gods love!

In Philippians 2:1 We are to imitate Christ, the Holy Spirit will help us share with others the message of Christ our Savior, "if any comfort from His love, if any common sharing in the Spirit, if any tenderness and compassion, then make my joy complete by being like-minded, having the same love, being one in Spirit and of one mind." It is because of Christ that we are saved, and the Holy Spirit will remind us to share all our love and peace with one another. The fellowship among believers is a common sharing produced by the Spirit of God who indwells in each of us.

We are like mined because we are of being of love sharing one mind to the other! We may not think alike but we have a uniformity of our thoughts.

Just recently we discovered a new TV channel that shows all of the Star-Trek series. When I saw Mr. Spock give a mind meld it reminded me of the same thing happening with the Holy Spirit. When Spock said, "My mind is like your mind; your mind is like my mind". Both minds become as one mind with each other. It is God's intention through the Holy Spirit for us to conceive his forming of the minds in order for each of us to indwell with a lasting fellowship and share with others within the Church family and staying in tune in-order to share our talents and gifts with one another; all for the good of the Church.

6

HELPING

f.   As His Helper: (Schema Israel): "Hear O Israel: I am about to send you a helper, "for the Lord God is one." (Duet: 6-4). A verse in (2 Corinthians 13-14), "The Grace of the Lord Jesus Christ and the Love of God and the Fellowship of the Holy Spirit are with all of you. Now that's what I call getting a prayer off to a good start.

In (Luke 1-35), "The Angel spoke to Mary, the Holy Spirit will come to help you, and the power of the Most High will over shadow you; and for that reason the holy Child shall be called the Son of God", you will name Him Jesus. Help comes from many directions and for many reasons? How would you like your day to start off with the booming voice of God! (Matthew 3:16-17), "as soon as Jesus Christ was baptized, he went up from out of the water. At that moment heaven opened, and He saw the Spirit of God descending like a Dove and landing on Him. And a voice from heaven said, 'This is my Son, whom I love; and with Him I am well pleased.'" The Holy Spirit will now stay with Christ, guiding Him and helping Him to fight off Satan as he prepares to enter the wilderness!

The presence of the Holy Spirit is needed in our daily lives, He can guide you and I as long as we call upon Him He will help us in all our tasks. The role of the Holy Spirit is different from Gods; He is to remind us of those things that God wrote on our hearts!

We can see in (Matthew 28-19), Jesus is about to send the disciples out to preach the good word and at the same time, He tells them I will send to them a helper that will come from the Father. Jesus said, "Go therefore and make disciples of all nations, baptizing them in the name of the Father and of the Son and of the Holy Spirit. This helping hand extended all the way to this present day, you and I are also responsible to do what Jesus our Lord commanded. Amen! The Holy Spirit will now be with them in all their endeavors!

God has placed in the Church men who will bear the gift of a helper not everyone can be an Apostle or a Preacher, so the gifts of those who can help within the church will be made know thru the Holy Spirit,(1 Corinthians 12).

Helping comes for us in many ways; like in James3:1-5 not many of us can be Teachers or Preachers, you should be aware that those who teach will be judge more closely by God. Mankind is capable of stumbling in many ways. If anyone does not stumble in what he says, he is then a perfect man, so able to bridle his whole body. If we put bits in the mouths of horses so that they obey us, we then are able to guide their whole body as well. Look at a large ship with or with-out sails, it is guided by a small rudder, controlled by a small person know as a pilot who directs the ship in its movements! Then there is the tongue it is a small member of the human body; yet it is able to boast of great things. Then there is a spark or a match such a as they can cause a fire that will burn down a forest. The tongue is very difficult to control; those who can control it can gain perfect control over the rest of their body; and all other area of their life.

7

INTERCEDING

g. (Job 16-20), "My intercessor is my friend, as my eyes pour out tears to my God ;(Verse 21) on behalf of a man He the Spirit pleads with

God as one who pleads for a friend". Job does not think he will live long enough to be vindicated before his peers? Everyone could see what was happening to Job in his life! Job knew this (Job 5-1) He knew he could rely on the Holy one of God; He would plead his case before God and himself! God would appoint a mediator an arbitrator that would give him satisfaction. This Holy one would be his intercessor the Holy Spirit (messenger) pleading his name to God! Jesus said "if you are ever arrested on false pretense concerning the word of God; don't worry about what to say, the Holy Spirit will talk for you". There are going to be times in your life that trouble will follow you no matter where or what it is, the life you live in Christ will carry you through. There will be a time in the End Times that these things will occur more than now. We must believe that the Holy Spirit of God will keep us safe to the point in that He will be right alongside of us and in our hearts always, interceding for us.

Oswald Chambers says, "Jesus carries on intercession for us in heaven; the Holy Spirit carries on intercession for us on earth; and we the Saints, have to carry an intercession for all men."

We as Saints do this by Praying for each other and for all things needed to have a Spiritual life in Christ! Do you remember in (Acts 12-5) Peter was in Prison and the Saints Prayed for him and as they were praying, Peter was knocking on the house door (Freed from Prison). To be anointed by the Holy Spirit (not by oil) but His filling your being with His Spirit; so that you can do things not thought possible! Christ is our intercessor in Heaven, the Spirit intercedes for us in our Hearts; God has provided for us the power of prayer with the Spirit.

Pray, Pray, and Pray for all things. In Ephesians 6:18, "Praying at all times in the Spirit, with all prayer and supplication." Prayer is a spiritual response and it can be either verbal, or unspoken? To supplicate is to pray earnestly, humbly, and beseechingly. It is a state of mind in order for us to request prayer or to be granted an answer to prayer! The Holy Spirit intercedes for us in all matters; His door is open and He eagerly awaits our heartfelt, soul-cleansing conversation so to speak.

CHAPTER 1   SUMMARY

The Holy Spirit is the greatest servant of God! When God spoke in the beginning the Spirit created all those things God wanted done!

At the day of Pentecost the Holy Spirit was visible as a flame of fire upon the heads of all persons there! You and I can receive the Spirit when we are baptized in the water, then you will be baptized by the Spirit by just asking God to give Him to you. The Spirit appeared to Christ as he was being baptized in the water then the form of a pure white Dove appeared and our Lord was considered to be baptized by the Spirit! Chapter one tells us of the seven ways of the servant of God!

1. How we are (Seeing) Him. We see him by Faith; in our lives the Spirit in us talks to the Holy Spirit of God for us thru Jesus. No one knows the thoughts of God except the Holy Spirit of God. For He indwells within us reading the things God has put on our hearts!

2. (Hearing) it is thru our Faith once again that the Holy Spirit will Speak to our heart as he indwells within us. One could be both blind and deaf; but he would still be able to hear and see the Holy Spirit within us.

3. (Giving) It's like having a bank account from heaven, we have been given automated deposit within us that won't go away; we can earn all kinds of interest on this account and even give or share it with others and still have plenty left!

4. (Correcting) Wow I wish I hadn't said that? We can't reach out with our tongue or our hands to retract the hurt full words we say. We can however rely upon the Holy Spirit to correct us to say the right words in the first place. We must have patience, think before we speak. Remember this; we must first ask and we will receive, seek in your heart and you will find the words. Knock and a door will open up for you to use the correct words.

5. (Sharing) All of mankind is prone to sin, but the Holy Spirit within us can help us to control our thoughts and actions. We must ask of Him and we will receive just what we need to share with others. The Holy Spirit can produce in us a clean heart, for he gives us love, joy, peace, goodness, gentleness, patience, kindness, faithfulness, and self-control. We have been enabled to reach into our hearts and use these eloquent spirit filled fruits.

6. (Helper) The helper of God for you and me! Remember this "Schema Israel"; I am about to send you a helper, "for the Lord God is one", But shared by the Father and the Son and the Holy Spirit. All are ready to fellow-ship with you were ever you go and whatever you do. It is the Holy Spirit that will travel with you along life's path-way.

7. (Intercessor) He intercedes as in Job 16-20, "My intercessor is my friend, as my eyes pour out tears to my God"! Job knew that God would not forget him and that there was a Spirit that would help him by going before the Lord as his witness to all that was going on in his life. You know Jesus will continue to intercede for you while He is in heaven and the Holy Spirit will intercede while on earth for us. Everyone should know that the Holy Spirit intercedes and corrects our words before they ever get to God. We have been anointed (not by oil) but thru the Holy Spirit that dwells within us to carry our prayers into the heavens so that God the Father Almighty can act upon them. As the Spirit intercedes for us, remember that when we pray we are interceding for others that are carrying heavy loads and they need your intervention with the Lords Spirit. Prayer is one of the best gifts we can give to one another!

ELEMENTS OF THE EARTH

THE SECOND OF
SEVEN STEPS

Chapter 2

———❧———

AS THE ELEMENTS OF SPACE AND EARTH

HOW DOES THE Holy Spirit use the Elements of the Earth; those that God had spoken to be in existent from the beginning as a gift to mankind! I thank God the Holy Spirit's use of these gifts of 1.- Wind, 2.- Water, 3.- Fire-, 4.- Oil, 5.- Air, 6.- Earth itself and 7.- Paper (parchment); as to glorifying the works of Father God! I thank Him for the wonderful Sunrise and the beauty of the Sunset's. Have you looked out on to the ocean lately, to see how its calming effect relaxes us? How about the moody seas that acts as our lives feel, sometimes good and sometimes not so good?

The beauty of the earth is seen with its changing seasons; like the Spring time it brings early rain so the flowers grow. Then the Summer time comes and we see the planted seeds covering the land and blooming to its full beauty. Then we see the time of Fall is for getting in the fruits of the seeds; winter time sets in, giving us yet another source of water, and time for the land to rest. Thank you Holy Spirit; for teaching mankind the ways to use his talents and gifts in caring for the earth. As I look up to the heavens I love seeing those elements; I.e. the planets, the moons, the constellations like the big dipper, little dipper; and the North Star and the Southern Star that will guide man to his destinations; In the air of space, on the seas, and traveling across the great land mass.

It is my intention to show that the Holy Spirit is just as real to me as the Son of God is! Jesus was serious when he said that he would ask the Father to send us a comforter an intercessor, one who will act in place of Jesus for all our days.

He will be with us always that are why I choose to be a little different in the way I show who He is. Remember in John 14-6 Jesus, said "I am the Way, the Truth, and the Life no one shall come unto the Father except by me". I believe that Jesus meant it for the Holy Spirit also! We know that the Father and Jesus are in each other and that the Spirit is in Jesus and the Father and all three are God. We can't see either of them, but they are just as real as the person standing next to you. The only difference is that it's by your Faith that the things you believe and Hope for, and you can't see are true. God created all of the elements and we have to believe that they all have a purpose for us on this Earth, and the Holy Spirit uses them to better our lives!

Do you remember the saying "Quench not the Spirit". He cannot be washed away, nor can He be hidden from us in any of the elements, but with the use of paper He can be made know to all those who are able to seek Him. There is a time when the Holy Spirit can be quenched; it is by us taking a wrong attitude? Whenever we reject the Spirits speaking to us from our hearts we treat Him with contempt and arrogance. Take the time to feel Him out just like a Policeman, or Fireman, before they go into action they stop and seek their inner training thoughts and then proceed with caution. Just like reinforced metal we need to be in the word of God each and every day of our lives. The Holy Spirit will support you in all of your endeavors!

The Gifts of the Holy Spirit bring us closer to understanding the uses of the elements of which God spoke into existence. Everyone has been given a talent, trade, or a gift to use while in this world; we should strive to put them to use for the betterment of your relationship within the confines of the Church; and for the betterment of your community!

In Galatians 3-2 "The blessings of Abraham thus come on all nations through Jesus Christ. Then both Jew and Gentile who have faith may receive the Spirit". The Bible treats the Holy Spirit as a distinct Person. He searches the hearts of all and any who seek Him to make intercession with Him.

1. WIND is our first element that we will look at. The wind as I have found in the Book of Acts; it is our 1st contact of the Holy Spirit in the lives of the Apostles. Therefore we should look for the feeling that they felt at Pentecost; it may not be felt by all, but the exaggeration of it is good.

2. **Water** ever since the creation this has been a profound statement: to include the Holy Spirit side of our God. He has been working to wash us all clean. Christianity is the foundation of Christ Jesus, showing us the way to be cleansed of our sins. With Jesus dying on the Cross and then we are to accept Him as the Son of God our Lord and Savior; and with each ones baptism this is sealing the effect of being ready to accept the help of the Holy Spirit.

3. When I received the Holy Spirit I felt like I was over heated but not burning up as with **fire**. I felt a comforting soothing feeling. A fire no less than the tongues of fire the Apostles and Disciples uncounted at Pentecost.

4. The effects of the anointing **oil** are what God intended for us to receive; in that we can go forth in this life and it justifies His Holy Spirits power. Many people seek a healing, forgiveness, and strength to move on in life.

5. With Gods breath of **Air** He will give us information that we will need and the Holy Spirit will relay that to Him what we say from our breath of air. Take a deep breath and be still, "that you may know that I am about to talk to you".(Psalms 46-10)

6. This **Earth** we live on is the Greatest of Gods achievements next to mankind. This earth was made for mankind to live and thrive on and with the use of its resources'. When we combine all of the elements of the earth we are well equipped to be provided for as long as we are alive on this earth.

7. How we accomplish the Great Commission as stated in Matthew 28-19; is because of the original parchment of **Paper** and today the very words of the testimony of the Apostles, Prophets, Evangelist, Preachers and Teachers of the words written down on paper; those from the Gospel of God!

The Seven Ways of the Elements

1

THE ELEMENTS OF WIND:

a. The Wind: The Apostles were told by Jesus to go to the upper room and wait for the Baptism of the Holy Spirit. They had been waiting for some forty days now, waiting and praying. They enjoyed each other's company and got to know each other a lot more than they had before. They participated each day in the remembrance of Jesus through the rites of the Last Supper! It would appear that the Spirit was working in their lives already blessing them and building them up for the task that they each would be sharing? While they were there; one named Matthias, was added to make twelve Disciples once again, since the death of Judas the one that betrayed Jesus!

I'm looking at the wind as a breath, a breeze or even air moving violently also Hebrew word Ruach for breath. In Isaiah 34:16 some scholars take the Spirit to mean (breath) since it is parallel with the (mouth). Some even feel that in Genesis 1:2 it was the Breath of God acting as the Spirit? It is said that the earth was void and without form and in the darkness a mighty wind blew and moved the water's. Then there is in Exodus 14:21; a strong west wind Kept blowing and keeping the river bottom dry until all Israelites could cross. The wind is invisible and so is the Spirit.

One cannot see it move or how it works? However, we can see the direction it comes and goes from by watching the elements around us; just by watching the trees and there branches we see movement. You don't see the wind itself, it is the same with the Holy Spirit; we get to watch people as they react to certain situations?

In (Gen 3:8 "The cool of the day", the Lord brought a cool breeze from the sea to the wilderness and with it the Quails to feed Gods people! In Jonah 1:4 the Lord sent a great wind when Jonah fled towards Tar shish? The Holy Spirit most likely is the wind and the breath, it seems most likely especially when we look at it God wants something done and the Spirit is the Great Servant of God!

In Genesis 7-22 there are two words associated with Spirit; (the Spirit of the Breath and of Life)? In this case the word Ruach was used?

In Genesis 8, God finally remembered Noah, and all the wild animals and the livestock, it was after 150 days when He sent the wind to move the flood waters and start a drying up process.

All thru the Old Testament the Holy Spirit appears to be thru Gods Power rather than a separate personality at times?

We must not equate that the Spirit in the Old Testament and the Holy Spirit in the New Testament are different from each other? With the people of the Old Testament God choose who He wanted for the Spirit to lead their lives! God gave them the Holy Spirit; they didn't have to ask for it. Today we ask for the Holy Spirit to come into our lives in our Baptism but we must ask God for Him! When we teach of Baptism of <u>Water</u> we need to teach that we must ask God to send the Holy Spirit to live in us. I like to teach, Lord let me receive the Baptism of the <u>Holy Spirit</u> fall fresh on me, mold me, melt me, make me like you? The Sacrament of Baptism whether it is by water or the Spirit changes you and when we receive it is then said that you have been baptized. This is an anointing that only you will feel, like the wind blowing a sweet smelling fragrance

MY HOLY SPIRIT

into your Heart and talking with the Spirit of your body given to you at, the moment of conception!

Think of the Holy Spirit coming into your Heart this way! The anticipation of His presence is absolutely wonderful. It's like looking into the Areola Borealis, at the North Pole (I was there it is beautiful) in the outer reaches of Alaska and the North Pole we hear the wind long before we feel it coming? Think of this when something in the kitchen is cooking and the smell is so great it makes your mouth watery, your tongue wants to taste this fragrance that works its way thru the air blowing like an easy wind to your sinuous!

The Spirit makes its way to your Heart thru your appealing of the stomach call. (The way to a man's heart is thru his stomach?)It is thru the Wind that gives us our first contact with the Holy Spirit (Noise) all of this happened before we fell the fire of the Holy Spirit (some say they don't experience their <u>Fire</u> of the Spirit) others do It is that tingling in your Mind, Heart and Soul. It was a rushing sound of the <u>Wind</u> that filled the <u>Air</u> of the upper room with the Apostles! The sound and wind made it fell like an Earthquake. The <u>Earth</u> felt like it was sliding like on <u>Oil</u> over a pond of <u>Water</u>. I thank God that they wrote all of this down on <u>Paper</u>.

We all should want to have the Peace of God in our Souls. We also want people to come to Christ and Gods Holy Spirit makes this possible for all who accept Jesus as the Son of God. Jesus gave us the Great Commission, "go forth and preach the Gospel to the entire world every people and every nation, and baptize in the Name of the Father and of the Son and the Holy Spirit."

2

ELEMENT OF WATER

b. The Water: Let us look back in time at the importance of water? When God asked that the earth be created, the Holy Spirit was given the task to remove the water from a blob that was without form! This water was put into a space between the now exposed lands of the earth, to a place of firmament of which God called the sky. God spoke to the Spirit and said let there be a light to shine during the day and He called this the Sun that would shine for all mankind. God said let there be a light between darkness and daylight and He said this would be called the Moon. This water was to be used by the not born yet mankind! Water would be for humans to drink, to feed the great forest and to feed the plants that would grow for mankind's sustenance in order to fill his belly? This water would trickle down from the exposed mountains that capture the water and freeze it like ice and snow then it would come down in streams and rivers as it melts to feed the great forest. The Forest would produce Oxygen needed for mankind to breath in the Air for him to survive! The Holy Spirit would then direct the Water to Ponds and Lakes were it would be stored to feed the great Pastures that would grow the sustenance for mankind to eat. It is said that 79% of the space on earth is water. Mankind uses the rest for habitat living! There are over 230,000 species that live in the water. Mankind's use of the element of water in the ocean and its food source of plant products, also produce specimens of life to make medicines to help retain life for mankind!

Let us look back to the Garden of Eden right up to Noah's time of the flood. Mankind was evicted from the garden because they committed sin, this very sin God will hold against mankind for a time

He chooses. The very Water that the Holy Spirit sent into the firmament above the earth was used to flood the Earth for 40 days and forty nights. This water took 150 days to recede to show the land again. God chose to flood the earth because mankind would not stop sinning, God promised not to do that again to wipe out all of mankind except for Noah's three sons and their wives and Noah's wife. God sealed His promised by putting a Rainbow in the sky to signify the rain would be stopping. The water that was the cause of the flood eventually evaporated to the firmament above; thus replacing it as in the beginning!

Water is known to be a cleansing agent; we know this from our baptism and its power, at the time of the First Century Christians baptism they did not receive the Holy Spirit automatically, God chose who he wanted to receive the Spirit! The water Jesus refers to includes three gifts, water that quenches the Spiritual thirst in us, it helps us to call upon the Spirit to talk to our birth spirit; it also helps us cleanse ourselves from the wrong things we have done in our lives? Remember again we are buried in the water of baptism, and rise up and lead a new life in Christ. We then ask God to send the Holy Spirit in to our lives to Guide us, this is done thru the water of our cleansing baptism! We do need baptism to wash away sin through baptism, the Holy Spirit enters into our hearts and here He begins the work of faith. As newborn Christians we start to live a new life that our Lord has planned for us; full of faith and service to one another and the Church. Baptism is a "means of grace" and it's the only way the Spirit can come to us in love to unite us with Christ! It also releases us from the death hold of our sins!

A Question comes to mind; I was asked how many times should I be Baptized? For those who were baptized at birth, I would say if you are not confident of your Baptism I would re-baptize you again. If you were baptized before you were an adult, and are having problems in life I would seek baptism again! Water baptism as Jesus; committed to with John the Baptist; was the example we needed to follow? Now Jesus Himself did not need to be baptized for the washing of sin, He was baptized for the priest-hood service He would be performing! There at His Baptism was the essence of what John said to the people," I baptize with water and there is one who will come after me and baptize you with the Holy Spirit". This most likely is why people fall away from the teaching of Christ, because they have not been introduced to the Holy Spirit? When Jesus rose up from the water, a pure white Dove came and landed on His shoulder, and then a booming voice from the Heavens above said, "This is my Son in whom I love". This of course would be the voice of God; showing us the presence of the Holy Trinity, The Father and the Son and the Holy Spirit!

Now let us take a close look at what Baptism Jesus was speaking of in Matthew 28-18-20; all authority of Heaven and Earth has been given me, therefore go and Baptize in the name of the Father, and of the Son, and the Holy Spirit. I go to the Father now but He will send to you what I promised you the Holy Spirit who will baptize you with Fire? The Holy Spirit is the key to a lasting and one time, never having to be baptized twice again! 1Corinthians 12-13 Paul said "for by one Spirit we are baptized into one body-whether Jews or Greeks, whether slaves or free-and have all been made to drink into one Spirit" The Apostle Paul said Cleary "there is one Lord, one Faith and One Baptism! If a person has repented and came back to the fold, they need not do it again! You remember the Prodigal son? He left the family, but they never stopped knowing or loving him?

If a person says he or she would like to be re-dipped again they have the mentality (of a very false doctrine) of being re-filled with the Holy Spirit; the Holy Spirit said He will be with us always and never leave us even into Heaven. Persons like this let themselves be very stale with God the Father, and what they really need is to believe they are in God's presence always and they can re-kindle the Flame of the Holy Spirit in them! Do not focus on the re-immersion; the way is thru the Baptism of the Holy Spirit.

Let the Holy Spirit fall fresh on you, let Him mold you; melt you into one who is always protected by God. Don't focus on being dunked or dipped in the tub of water, instead focus on being immersed with the flame of the Holy Spirit! (Ephesians 1:13, 4:30, 5:5.)

Consider this (John 4-13) Jesus used water in a figurative sense; Jesus said to the woman at the well, "drink of this water and you will still thirst". But, "whoever drinks of the water I shall give him will never thirst."

MY HOLY SPIRIT

3

ELEMENT OF FIRE

c. Element of Fire brings on the effect of the Holy Spirit. Sometimes we can look at the Holy Spirit of the Old Testament (O.T.) and try to compare Him with the Holy Spirit of the New Testament (N.T.), but in fact He is the same in both the Old and New Testaments! The difference is explained in this way? God gave Him to those He chose in the O.T.; and in the N.T. we must call upon Him to receive Him, we ask in this manner, Oh Holy Spirit of God come into our lives to comfort us and to lead us to the path that seeks Jesus our Lord and Savior! The Pentecostal experience is in fact what we look for as we receive Him! The Holy Spirit of God is the same today as He was yesterday or in the old days.

The day of Pentecostal out pouring actually connects with the O.T. experience as well as the O.T. promise. On this day we can see the accumulation of the O.T. harvesting of the saints who believed. It was the long awaited day of the Church of God! There was a sound in the Heavens like thunder and lightning then a mighty feeling of a strong rush of wind. But there was no actual wind; it was the sound that filled the upper room of the house where the Apostles were. It was more than the breath of a wind as in the O.T. saints thought that brought in a new life. Then it happened; what appeared was like cloven tongues of fire and it sat on each one's head that was in the room. These tongues of fire were distributed evenly upon each saint in the upper room. It was like watching most likely a ball of fire coming out of the ceiling it divided itself into separate tongues to sit upon each saint's head

These were people filled with the love of God, and open to the teaching of Jesus Christ. They have already been cleansed in the baptismal waters; and now they are being baptized with the Holy Spirit. Remember at Jesus baptism in (Mt: 3-16) He was baptized with the water and the Holy Spirit at the same time. When this happened Jesus rose up out of the water and a pure white dove came and sat on His shoulder this dove represented the Holy Spirit of God and then there was a thunder in the clouds and the voice of God spoke saying "this is my Son; whom I love, with Him I am well pleased". Here we can see that the Father and the Son and the Holy Spirit were all present at the same time thus proving the formation of the Holy Trinity!

In Acts 1-8 we are told that Jesus said for the Apostles, they were to go to the upper room and wait for the Fire of the Holy Spirit. Soon after Jesus spoke these words he rose on a cloud to the Heavens above.

The fire we receive today at our Spiritual Baptism is a feeling or sensation of doing well to each other. It is like an experience of great enthusiasm; it's a dedication of the gifts we receive from the Holy Spirit! Jesus tells us it's like receiving Power to serve others. Jesus gave us the Great Commission that we should go into the whole world and preach the word of God and baptize all who believe that Jesus is the Son of God. If there is any one thing we can take with us to those who are sinners as we all are; it's this Baptize them with the fire of the Holy Spirit for it is like sanctification or more of purification to each believer. Each of us receives something a little different; but we are all dead to sin and we are alive with the fire of the Holy Spirit. The fire is applied with the boldness we take in believing we are filled with the Holy Spirit!

4

ELEMENT OF OIL

d. What can the oil of anointing do for us? Why does God accept us? How can we meet His perfect standards? Maybe you have a hard time believing that God accepts us unconditionally! With the use of the anointing oil in a proper manner we may be able to see this is the answer?

In the book of Samuel He shows us how God has selected those He choose to be anointed with the oil and the Spirit? Now we don't know if Samuel himself was anointed with the oil but he was filled with the Holy Spirit; if we go back in time when he was dedicated at the Temple he would have been filled with the Holy Spirit; then he would be able to fulfill Gods mission for his holy life! God called Samuel to use the anointing oil in the Book of 1 King (1-34) and 2 Kings (9-3).

God showed Moses the need for the oil in the anointing of the Levite Priest in the book of Exodus (30-30), Leviticus (8-30). This oil was a special blending of Herbs and spices mixed gently with olive oil! The ingredients were as follows (in case you might want to make your own?) 1. Stacte, a sweet spice to make incense. 2. Onycha, a nail of a snail found in the Red Sea. 3. Galbanum, an aromatic bitter resin or fennel substance. 4. Frankincense, aromatic resin from Boswellia trees. 5. Olive oil, fat obtained from the olive, (this was fifty percent of the anointing oil.

The use of the anointing oil is for God's purpose, His servants, and beautifying oneself. It is used for healing, dedicating officials of God and things of God (I: E :) furniture, pianos, organs and whatever is given or donated to the Church for Gods purpose.

I believe that if one is anointed for the talents they have, they will be able to share the use of them with others. This is to assure that they will not lose the talents that were given to them.

Oil is very special to God! Try this put oil on your hands even suntan oil then dip your hands into water, see the water runoff? Well this is what happens to the trials and tribulations of our lives when we are anointed with the oil! The effects and uses of the anointing oil can be boundless. Moses was instructed by God to anoint Aaron and all the Priest of the Levite order, they were to be washed with their garments on in the water as in Baptism; just as Jesus did with John the Baptist in the Jordan River.

This particular Baptism (if you will) is the acceptance of the Priest of Israel and then they would be anointed with oil and the Spirit would come into them to perform their duties in accordance with Gods Holy Word! It would be the power of God working in them to do His bidding.

Samuel anointed Kings Priest and Judges; He anointed Saul, David and Isaiah was also anointed to all do the work of God thru the Holy Spirit. All those that were anointed were done so that they would be set apart of all other men, so that their Ministry would thrive.

This anointing with oil; by Moses and Samuel and all the O.T. Prophets I believe was not to be imitated; its uses beside to anointing of the people chosen, was also used to anoint all things within the Temple. Today as in the past we anoint all things with in the Temples or the church. Some things like the Piano, Organ and any equipment that is donated or give to the Church for Gods purpose. Oil continues to this day to be the symbol of the Holy Spirit.

5

ELEMENT OF AIR

e.   The Holy Spirit breaths on mankind with air softly felt, very warming and giving to us the feeling of the His presence. With mankind the breath of air that comes out of our mouth is formed with words that are pushed out with our tongue. This can be heard by others. With the Holy Spirit it's not sounds we recognize as hearing of words, but that of a feeling inside that we are being talked to by an invisible spirit! We can say upsetting things at times? If we confess with our mouths that Jesus Christ is Lord, this is a good thing and we need to say only good things by asking the Spirit to aid us in all things that come out of our mouths. The Holy Spirit breaths into us to say the correct things, we must listen to our hearts before we say anything! If we confess from our mouths (Rom: 9-10) that Jesus is the Son of God we should be able to see in our hearts the road of salvation put in front of us.

God spoke and the Spirit performed, He caused the water to move to the firmament above which God called the sky. It was the breath of air that moved the water something like the wind ever so strong moving twenty-five percent of the water to be put in reserve for a later time. Have you ever watched a whale come to the surface and excrete the stale air inside of him; it comes out with such great force; this water spout it forms could move a three ton truck straight up in the air. The Holy Spirit can give us that same feeling of power as we excrete the air from inside us only thing, it is formed by the tongue into words that can hurt or give forth love!

The Holy Spirit will show us in our hearts and mind those words we seek to please others. We must be conscious of the breath we let out or take in. The Bible tells us the Spirit is God and that He is visible not only inside of us, but in our outward actions. (In 1 Corinthians 6-19) "We are the temple of God"; we are not ourselves alone we should do all things recommended by the Holy Spirit. We should not be ashamed that what we declare from our mouths that exalt God's word, which is given to us by His Spirit.

I must have read John 15-26, John 16-12 and all of John 17, several times one day and I got this message! Jesus had to leave this earth because He had completed His mission given to Him by the Father. We would be granted Salvation thru God's Grace, and Jesus would be sanctified and God would be glorified. Jesus did leave us these promises, He would ask the Father to send us a helper, and counselor, comforter, redeemer, and He will be known as the Spirit of Truth. When we ask for the Holy Spirit to come into our lives He will breathe on us and give us the words of truth that will speak to our hearts. He then will interpret for us all we are able to speak from our hearts and our mouths. Any message or prayer we say with earnest, He will pass on to God the Father exactly what God wants to hear from the breath of our mouths.

In each of us there is a breath of hope, we need to step back and listen to the Holy Spirit as He talks to us thru our inner heart. When He talks to us it's like a puff of air so sublime it is only felt in our hearts! Think of it this way; you are flying a kite and it goes out of sight, but you feel the tug of it thru the string, and you know that it is still there, just as His Spirit is within us.

6

ELEMENT OF EARTH

f. The uses of the Earth, is like going back to the beginning book of Genesis. The Holy Spirit the greatest servant of God did what all that was asked of him to do. He exposed the land, valleys, hills, forest and even the mountains. He then exposed the streams, rivers, pounds and the lakes for they are all a part of the earth that was uncovered when a portion of the water was removed and placed in the firmament above called the sky. God loved all that was created and said it was very good. He did all this for the coming of mankind, that he would have sustenance to live on.

The land would be put to use for mankind to grow his crops to produce foods that would feed his kind. This new land would have nutrients in the soil to add to man's diet.

The valleys would be where most of God's creatures would live. Man was made from the dust of the earth and woman from the bone of man; God put them together to be as one and to propagate the world.

The hills and the valleys would be where the Spirit would locate mankind to live in suitable comfort. In buildings made of wood from the trees.

The beautiful green forest, were created to produce oxygen that all creatures would be able to breathe air that would fill their lungs. It also would provide lumber to build houses and building and bridges.

The mountain's at the high places the water would settle and freeze, and would catch the snow and it would melt and trickle down the mountain side.

This trickling of water would form streams and waterfalls, even rivers of water that would be captured in lakes and ponds to be used by mankind.

He would use it for drinking and to feed the plants that he would grow for his sustenance. Even the oceans of the world are now made visible to man and they would produce sea life that mankind would use to feed himself.

The land of the earth that the Spirit exposed is the culmination of God's creation that all life shall begin. We are now begging to see the works and organization of God's extremely beautiful earth. This earth is made for mankind not mankind for the earth!

Gods Spirit gave us a home forever even when the Earth gets renewed as I n revelations 21-1, "I saw a new Heaven descend on a new Earth", the Apostle John saw this vision at the end of time.

The water trickled down the mountains in streams so that it could feed the great forest below that would produce the oxygen we would need to breathe the air given to us thru the Spirits ways. These streams would turn into rivers and they would collect in the lakes that would store the water for use in the future or as we would need it! The water would then be channeled to feed the valleys that the pastures and gardens would grow for mankind's sustenance in order to feed his body. Then there is the water of the Ocean's created by God's Holy Spirit that would further feed mankind with ample resources of fish life, plus the vegetation of the Ocean that will help mankind in the medical field. The holy Spirit helps us use all of the resources of this earth not only the growing of food, the use of the ocean, the use of the trees of the forest that can also be used to gather or for mankind to hunt for his food. There is an old Indian saying here in Alaska, (P.S. I'm on vacation in Alaska Sitka to exact and I have found this quote from the Indian village quite interesting.) "Save this for the children forever and ever."

Translated from the Indian language that reads as this ("Haa ya-txi Gaye-is Aye"). This can also mean "The Spirit provides till the end of time."

As long as mankind lives with a flesh and blood body he will be responsible to care for the earth. The Holy Spirit will lead mankind in ways to care for this earth of Gods choosing. It is when mankind goes against the uses of the elements of the earth he is at the mercy of his mistakes.

In the book of Revelations, it says a time will come when mankind will be so against each other the land will suffer and the blood will flow.

In the end times the land will suffer it will surely be abused. When the end comes for mankind the earth, and all that is within it will be destroyed. What God saw as very good after the creation; Geneses 1-1 "In the beginning God created the heavens and the earth." Now in Revelations 21-1, "I saw a new heaven descend on a new earth."

Yes after mankind makes a mess of this earth that we know our maker God will destroy the earth with a cleansing fire. This will wipe out all those things that mankind has made or constructed to his delight. God's new heaven will set on a newly refined earth and He will dwell with man forever!

7

ELEMENT OF PAPER

g. The use of Paper as in Parchment writing was the way to speak to one another in centuries past. It is the most versatile tool to converse with one another for thousands of years. You can print or write or stamp on it, as it made an impression that was visible to the eye. Printing on paper by electronics as a typewriter, computer or printing press is the modern way. As of 1454 someone named Gutenberg printed the very first Bible that would be available to all mankind.

Some of the early years before 202BC paper like rice paper or parchment paper was found in the caves in jars, were to have been first invented by China. The method, of writing on objects before the Chinese would have been on stone, bamboo, or bones, tree products or even on cloth like silk or rags; were to have been used well before paper, remember God wrote on tablets of stone! In the times of Pharaoh they wrote on both paper and stones.

What better way is there to preserve the word of God!

In order to use paper or paper products we need to cut down the tree's that produce the oxygen we need to breathe. We find that when we use one element we actually end up using two elements in order to use just one. When water moves over the ground as in floods, erosion takes place of the land. When we have drought's the lakes dry up and the life in them dies off? When a fire occurs in the forest or our homes there is a loss of trees and shelter for mankind and the excessive use of water to put the fires out.

The Holy Spirit guides us in the use of the elements so that we must be careful not to use more than one element at the same time.

How is it I can use paper as a separate element of the earth? It is one that can be explained as coming from the Spirit of God that it is His way of breathing into mankind to write down on paper or parchment those words He wants us to see as well as hear. In Revelations we see the stories of the seven churches, and Jesus says he who has an ear them hear my words, this was all written down for us to see and to hear it from someone's mouth. There are those that can't read but they can hear, thank God for the touch of Braille so that the blind may see the word and hear it also!

There is a story I like to tell, it's about ten men in a room and they are asked to pass on a statement that was written down, the first man was to whisper in the next man's ear, this is what he read to pass on, (the gifts of the Holy Spirit have many different values) and he was to pass the information on. The fourth man was to write down what he heard before he passed the saying on He heard this and wrote on a piece paper these words,("the holy Spirit will's us each day to pray"). He then passed that on, and the eighth man was to write down what he heard before he passed it on, ("the Spirit will be expected to pray for us").He then passed that on and the tenth man was expected to recite what he heard. He said this, ("If you are expecting pray"). What happened, when you compare this to what was originally said, and written down on paper what do we see? Let's compare the first original one, "The gifts of the Holy Spirit have many different values", and the last one; "If you are expecting pray". What I see here, as long as we have the written word in front of us we shouldn't be able to lose what God wanted us to see or hear; whether it's God the Father or Jesus the Son or the Holy Spirit of God! They are all working in our temple, the temple of God our Bodies!

When Jesus read from the Torah in the temples He was doing what God requested Him to do. He quoted from the Torah that which God wanted us to hear, and remember. The written word was established by God the Father Almighty; He said to Moses write down these things and events that happened that the future world will see them, and we do till this day.

Paul wrote in Acts 20-32, "my brothers I commend you to God for the words of His grace". The very essence of God's word will sustain each of us every time we read the word of God. When we share His word we not only educate ourselves but others as well. The Holy Spirit bears witness to our spirit, we are then able to build up an inheritance in reading His word and thereby we can be sanctified thru them. The Spirit tells us we are the children of God, we suffer with Jesus that we may be glorified thru Him and He has Glorified Himself to the Father, and the Father is glorified because of the works of the Son.

In 1 Peter 1, we see that all flesh is like grass, and the glory of mankind is like a flower in the grass; when the grass dies off the flower falls apart. But in (v-25) "the word of the Lord endures forever, and this is the word, which by His gospel is preached." When we all get to heaven the word of God will still be made available to us. The word of God will not be forgotten even thou a new heaven will descend on a new earth as in Revelation 21-1. Remember this all that has been written on paper, parchment or scrolls has been afford to you, and those who believe that the Son of God is Jesus; as the Holy Spirit has talked to your spirit that His holy word can be trusted. The gospel is for your salvation, believe in it and you will be sealed with the Spirit as Promised. One of my favorite verses is in Psalm 119-105, "Thy word is like a lamp unto my feet, and a light unto my path."

CHAPTER 2   SUMMARY:

We have looked at the elements of the earth as I have seen them, especially those mentioned in the Book of Genesis. The Holy Spirit uses these elements for our purpose that we might understand the purpose of God. God wanted mankind to be comfortable in his surroundings; I guess if He wanted us to all be fish He could have left the water right where it was. I'm glad that he made us who we are. I like the wind blowing in my hair and breathing the fresh air of the cool mountains. I just love looking up into the sky where His fingers arranged all of the stars and planets and the constellations.

1.   The element of the Wind is surprisingly a product of the Holy Spirit of God. (Ps 104-15) "He makes the wind His messenger".

      (Mt 24-31) "He gathers His elect from the four winds". I look at the wind as a breath of air. In John 3-8, we are told that "the wind blows from were ever it pleases". We don't see the wind or the Holy Spirit, but we see how people act and we see the trees move from the effect of the wind, (Holy Spirit). In the Great Commission Jesus made the Holy Spirit available to all disciples (you and I), to go forth and preach the Gospel and to Baptize all who believed that Jesus was the Son of God.

2.   The element of Water! Once again starting in the Book of Genesis we see the use of the Holy Spirit moving the water as in the creation and taking a portion of it and putting it in the sky above. Then we see how he directs the water over the mountains and down the paths as rivers to the valleys below only to settle in lakes and ponds, so that mankind can put it to use. Then we see how He used the water to flood the earth again in Noah's time. The Spirit once again removed the water as the wind to put it back in the sky above.

      We know that water acts as a cleansing agent, especially in baptism, once the water is used to sprinkle or to immerse someone we find that we have baptized them. We have been considered to be buried with Christ and emerge to rise again and lead a new life in Jesus Christ.

3. The element of Fire was visible at Pentecost, with the flames dotting about on the heads of all those that were in the room that had accepted Jesus as the Son of God. These people were filled with the love of Gods Holy Spirit. The effects of fire is applied with a boldness we take in believing we ask for the Holy Spirit and it will feel like a very warm sensation as being in a fire.

4. The element of Oil for Christians and like others is the anointing we receive in accepting the Holy Spirit. There is a specific formulary that is followed to make the oil holy and to have the anointing be believable and its effect will take hold for the purpose it was done for. I mentioned that we can anoint things that will be donated to God for His church to use them in worshiping Him.

5. His Spirit is like a fresh Breath of Air to be felt ever so gently. In receiving the Holy Spirit it's not by sounds, or sight that we feel the Spirit but it is like a warm feeling inside of us that gently tugs at our heart. We thank God for the Spirit He has given each of us when we were born. Our Spirit needs guidance, that's when we call upon Him to come into our hearts and lead us as a puff of air so sublime it is only felt in our hearts.

6. The use of the Earth itself is one of the primary elements found in the Book of Genesis that point out mans need of the Earth, Air, Water, Wind, and even Fire. These were the original elements. The earth is the dirt of the land, the mountains and the valleys that mankind would dwell on and produce his sustenance in order to live.

7. The forest that would produce the oxygen that mankind would need to breathe the air to fill his lungs to live.

    His use of the word paper or parchment, how else would we be able to get His word to us. Paper was Gods choice and each Spirit lead person who was asked to write down the word of God felt Him breathe into them what He wanted them to say. There was the story of the ten men in a room all asked to pass on a phrase or statement that was whispered into one ear at a time we saw when the last person got the message it was not even close to the original message. So we have paper written down as long as the original paper is not lost we can be assured that what was to be heard will be what God wanted passed on.

The Holy Spirit guides us in the use of all of the elements, and we must use caution when we use more than two elements at the same time. For instance we cut a tree down for wood or making paper but we destroy its use to produce oxygen. So what do we do we replant a new tree in its place. Remember my favorite verse in the Bible is found in Psalm 119-105, "thy word oh Lord is like a lamp unto my feet, and a light unto my path".

HIS POWER

THE THIRD OF SEVEN STEPS

Chapter 3

———— ❧ ————

THE POWER OF THE HOLY SPIRIT.

As I TRY to explain the task of the Holy Spirit I find it is not an easy task; but remember this He is God incarnate. God is the Father, Jesus, and Holy Spirit, (all of one and all by one). The trinity was of God separating into, three persons, and chosen by Him-self, God. It is not like the Three Musketeers (all for one, one for all).

Who gives the Father, the Son and the Holy Spirit the Power they have? The answer should be the triune God. This being the case is the power of the Holy Spirit equal to that of God. My Wife's answer is this, "if He gets His power from God the power cannot be equal!" When you share something with anyone you still have control. What I say is this we must remember that it is His, Gods Spirit that He is sharing and He (does) act as Himself, and as the Father and the Son and the Holy Spirit, God is One, and He controls all aspects of who He is; otherwise He would not be God.

1. I believe that Faith in any subject matter of God is the truth as He has revealed it to us in scripture. "We live by faith and not by sight".

(2 Corinthians 5-7) When we look in a mirror we see our-selves, but not as God see's us. Our Faith comes to us in belief of His holy word. We won't really know all the truths of our Faith until the day Jesus returns for us

2. He will cater to our every Need as in (Matthew 7-7),"Ask and you will receive, seek and you will find, knock and the door will be opened." This is in line with the insistence of the Positive Power of Prayer. We are to pray always often and thru the Holy Spirit.

3. The Sovereignty of the Holy Spirit is established in Genesis 1: 1-27 in the creation of which God had the Holy Spirit perform in all acts to establish the earth as a live-able place for mankind that is to come. The Holy Spirit acts for us as well as He acted in obeying God's commands. We are too a new creation of God's and all we have to do is ask for His help.

4. The Holy Heavenly Spirit acts for God and is our reminder to obey the commands of Jesus .All those inner most thoughts written on our hearts that Jesus taught to His Apostles will be revealed to us through the Spirit as we ask for them.

5. He also acted for Jesus, in making mankind in their image, in the image of God, both male and female! We will look in the book of Hebrews how man's faith may help him in his longevity.

6. The Holy Spirit does these things as He indwells within us at our heart.

For those of us who believed that we were re-born, when we were baptized in the water; And did receive the Holy Spirit as we asked for Him to indwell in our hearts; and lead us in a new life as Jesus received Him at His baptism. We then started a life in discipleship for our Lord and Savior with the Spirit in our Hearts.

7. He molds us to be like Jesus and for us to obey as He has obeyed God the Father in all He has done. Our God wrote on our hearts

all those things He wanted us to know and do, it is the Holy Spirit that will bring them out as (we) ask Him to.

Jesus' disciples (Acts 2-38) also believed in the assurance of receiving the Power of the Holy Spirit at the day of Pentecost. Their waiting made them stronger in faith and in their relationship with each other. The eleven were not alone in that room there were other disciples there and up to 120 others all of which received the Holy Spirit. Everyone received the same blessing as the eleven, each one believed, even though they did not see. I say this; they believed that they had a new reborn life as it came to all the disciples in that room.

The Holy Spirit of God reminds us that we are a new creation in Jesus the Christ. We are His workmanship and have the mind set of our Lord and Savior. We are to put off the old self and put on the new self and be thankful to God for His Grace and Salvation.

The Seven Ways of the Holy Spirits Power:

1

THE POWER OF FAITH

a.   The use of His Power of Faith; Faith is of our believing and not by being able to see it. How do you respond to something unseen? How many different ways does it need to be presented to you before you believe? Do you have the doubting Thomas syndrome? These three questions deserve three good answerers. I will give the answers in looking at a few people of the bible that were endowed with the Holy Spirit.

I would like us to look at Moses' sister Miriam. She had a great impact on the Israelites! Miriam was established as a Prophetess and she was made a Judge of Israel under Moses reign. She led the women of Israel in music and praise (Judges 4:4-6). She was filled with the Holy Spirit as was Aaron and Moses! Miriam's ministry however was cut short, as she was very jealous of her brother Moses. She felt that she deserved more than what the Holy Spirit gave to her? Then God had her struck with Leprosy, but after seven days He took it away from her! Her ministry abruptly ended until her death.

It is possible that acts of faith and obedience can be lost when we do not seek that which God has given to us so freely. She did well as a prophetess and a judge but she lost her faith in what she was doing for the betterment of God's people. She became focused on herself and what she thought she should have, and not the Spirit's way.

(Romans 1-17) "For there is the righteous of God revealed from faith to faith: as it is written, they should live by faith".

Now we will look at two men that God gave the Holy Spirit to and took it away, but the Spirit returned to them to accomplish what God needed to be done; in spite of what they had did wrong. We look at Jepthah and Samson. Israel has always been a backsliding nation; they used and practiced whatever spiritual beliefs of the nations they occupied. This upset God very much! This caused them to lose whatever moral and spiritual values they were taught.

Jepthah replaced his father in ruling the kingdom his Mother was known as a "scared prostitute", (Judges 10-6-7) it was Jephthah brother who ran him out of Israel for his bad conduct he managed to lose the Spirit and it was obvious. He was called back to fight against the Amorites and was promised he could rule again only if God wanted him to? The Holy Spirit did come upon him and gave him a victory only after he made a foolish promise to God if he won the battle. He said I promise that the first one who comes out of the door of his house after he returns in celebration I will sacrifice to you. When he returned home the first one out of the house was his only daughter for he had no son. This was heart breaking, his daughter said not to worry honor the pledge to God , but first let me have two months of freedom as I will be a virgin and never be able to marry. The Holy Spirit granted this and he lived six more years as the ruler of Israel.

Samson was another anointed by the Holy Spirit to lead in battle against the Philistines. An Angel of the Lord came to his Mother saying you will bear a child and you are to not drink any wine or fermented liquids, or eat any unclean foods (Judges 15 & 16). The Angel told her that he will be raised as a Nasserite and his hair shall not be cut.

Samson fornicated with many women and killed many Philistines warriors in proved attacks. Then he meets Delilah and four times she was bribed to get the secret from him about his strength. It was not until the fourth time that he lost his strength, but not because of the loss of his hair, it was because the Holy Spirit departed from him. He was then captured and had his eyes gouged out. He was made to be a common laborer. In time his hair grew back and he prayed and pleaded to God to restore his strength and to let him die with all those that he will bring down. He brought down the temple of the Philistines with thousands in it; his body was recovered and taken home for burial. Hair was not the reason for his strength; it was the indwelling of the Holy Spirit that gave him his strength and a precocious attitude of using the Spirit. We need Him as our guide and it requires us to be ever diligent in our actions. We must believe that the Spirit will take care of all our needs, and not to go out on our own without consulting Him first.

Jephthah and Samson were examples of losing the Spirit and then gaining back His trust and favor with the Lord once again. The Holy Spirit did return to them (I do not believe that the Spirit actually left them He was silent) in order to accomplish what the Lord wanted done.

Now here (Judges 4 & 5) is an excellent example of being led by the Spirit and it is found I believe in a woman who had much faith, named Deborah that she has found the favor of God. He put the Holy Spirit in her to lead as a Judge of Israel! Deborah was not chosen because of her military might but for her loving and understanding ways. In the Jewish Talmud which is a dictionary of Aramaic history, it spoke of the judges being filled with the Spirit! They had a history of heroism, ruled somewhat fairly, and restrained the people from idolatry. We are also given the things of wisdom and knowledge, in their Judging and rescuing them for salvation and redemption. Deborah actually held court under the shade of a Palm tree .People had faith in her as they came to her with their problems, disputes or questions. Her judging of the people was favorable with them and she was filled with the Spirit. Deborah was having a problem with the Canaanites, she appointed an Army Commanding General Barak; at first he would not go against the Canaanites unless she went with him. She said she would be right by his side, but he would not get credit for the victory, but she a woman would get credit. The Spirit decided all aspects of the battle and Deborah got the credit. Barak recognized she was filled with the Spirit.

Deborah new she was filled with the Spirit and made the verse in 1 Corinthians 6-19 more understanding to us now; "What? Know you not, that your body is the temple of the Holy Spirit which is in you, that which came from God, and it is not your own body"?

We do walk by faith when we listen to the Spirit as He talks to us, for "without faith it is impossible to please Him, for those who come unto God must actually believe that He is God who rewards those that diligently seek Him". (Hebrews: 11-6).

Remember this, today in our era, the Holy Spirit comes to those who ask for Him and there are those, that God chooses who should receive Him. For it is Gods choice to send Him no matter what it will be for. It is His glory that His wonderful works are assigned.

2

OUR NEEDS:

b.   Catering to our Needs; that may be hidden?

Needs are like obligations, to be filled with something we lack. I see three areas of needs, the first is the need of Courage, then there is Patience, and the need of Peace. These are what we can expect the Holy Spirit to fulfill to satisfy our desires that fill our hearts and minds with the love of God. (Like Fruits of the Spirit)

The simple definition would be the ability to conquer our fears and or despairs! In Philippians 4-6 we find this quote," Be careful for nothing, but in everything by prayer and supplication, with thanksgiving let your request be made known unto God."

If we do not pray to have our fears taken away we can have a very despairing life. It is the work of the Holy Spirit to take all our fears away so that we may lead a life in love and understanding. Our need to take fear away requires courage and that comes thru the Spirit. Satan can plant in your mind nasty tales about yourself and if you start to believe them your fears can come true. The Holy Spirit can cure our fears, He will cleanse us of the bad dreams, and He will most definitely Care for us so that our hearts will be free to accept Him as we need Him.

In Isaiah 43-2 we see this," when thou passes' threw the waters, I will be with thee; and through the rivers, and they shall not over flow thee: when thou walk through the fires, thou shall not be burned, neither shall the flame kindle upon thee."

If we can do anything thru Christ we surely can expect the Holy Spirit to be able to accomplish this caring for our needs of courage?

Our courage will lead us to be in a free state of mind thru our belief of faith in the Holy Spirit. Our hearts will feel the gentle nudging that will release all our woes and we will walk in the Spirit.

The Spirit will also help us to find patience in our quest to find the freedom to set us free from worries.

I have heard that it is Jesus' Holy Spirit that indwells within us. I say this that in us is the Spirit of all things he has done and those we remember of Him. We should note that Jesus is God as the Father is God and the Holy Spirit is God; each one the chosen one of God and separate of each other as God is one so is the Spirit, Jesus and The Father. At Pentecost the Holy Spirit came to them and indwelled to all who were there. It was an earth shattering event more than Christmas? What I'm saying is this, God came down to us and became man! Now with the Spirit God is inviting us to be a child of God and offering us a chance to have eternal life.

Just recently the Pastor of our Church held a thirty day Power of Prayer, Praise, Patience of supplication, and the inner Peace of our testimonies session. During those days we sang the song "Trust and Obey", each and every day. We must trust in the power of the Holy Spirit He will give us what we Need; (Courage), and he will see to it that we have control of our Patience and it will give us a Peace that will lead us to our spiritual freedom in our walk of this life.

Are you ready to welcome the Spirit into your life? He waits for you to call upon Him as He is omnipresence within you just call for Him! (Hebrews 10-36, "for your need of patience, is to do the will of God, that you might receive the promise". Make the Holy Spirit welcomed into your Heart today and always. In 1 Corinthians 1-10 Paul tells us, "I'll put it to you as urgently as possible: you must get along with each other. You must learn to be considerate with one another, in order to cultivate a life in common with one another".

This will build up strength to meet any temptation that may come along in your walk of this life. In your prayer life will you wait patiently and quietly for your answer no matter the time it takes.

When we have learned to accept the things we need like courage of strength for our fears; and the endurance of long lasting patience, we must remember that it is of the fruits of the Spirit that we can see not only these things but an everlasting Peace. The Spirit gives us all these things, Love, Peace, Patience, Goodness, Gentleness, Kindness, Joy, Faithfulness, and Self-control! He is after all the Spirit of Truth in all matters, sent by God at the request of Jesus. He is to fill all our needs; He is our comforter, redeemer, and our interpreter.

Let us never forget that we are the Spirit filled children of God the Father Almighty. We are bound to glorify God with our bodies as they belong to God.

3

His Sovereignty

c.   He reigns with all truth in all matters. It is the Spirit that gives us wisdom and then applies it to our hearts. We are to be encouraged by the fact that we may never feel the need to be afraid of anything as long as the Spirit is within us. We are to obey what he puts on our hearts and He will not lead us astray! Remember we talked about Him being the element as the wind? Well we can't see Him for sure but we can hear Him and Feel Him as the wind. Sometimes He is subtle enough He is like a tug on the heart! Or He can do like He did at Pentecost pricking the hearts of many. No matter what the timing or the situation He consults no one He comes at a time of His choosing after we ask for Him. He is the sovereign one to give us new birth of our Spirit.

MY HOLY SPIRIT

We will take another look at the trinity as it is referenced to our salvation. God the Father predestined us to receive Him, God the Son is our propitiation of favor, and the Holy Spirit is our regeneration for our new life. For God so loved the world and anyone who accepted His Son, would be redeemed for long life.

The Holy Spirit's purpose is to give us re-birth; He alone has sovereignty that we should be "Born of the Spirit".

God the Father has predestined all those He wants to receive God the Spirit; The Spirit then seeks out those that were chosen. It will be a Spiritual resurrection and not of our choosing. The Spirit causes us to lead a new life in Christ Jesus; we will be sanctified and receive salvation through God's grace.

Have you come into favor with our Lord God Almighty? In Isaiah 61-1 "The Spirit of the Sovereign Lord is upon me, because the Lord has anointed me to proclaim good news to the poor and has sent me to bind-up the brokenhearted; and to proclaim freedom for the captives and release from darkness those prisoners." This is an insight as to what Jesus said for the commissioning of the Apostles and disciples to go out into the world and proclaim the Gospel of the Lord! It will be thru the Spirit that this proclamation will be accomplished!

The Holy Spirit is sovereign in all matters of our lives, needs, commissions, evangelical works, in our everyday comforts; He will guide us to all truths and will give us visions of our needs for the future. He confirms the very fact that Jesus had to die for us on the cross otherwise we all would be lost in our quest for eternal life!

In Romans 8: 5-8, I see that mankind has two mindsets; one is the flesh, we tend to do whatever it takes to satisfy our pleasures in life. This is not the way to the kingdom of God? Let's call it the sins of the flesh that will only lead us to deaths road. On the other hand there is the Holy Spirits way, thru all the fruits of the Spirit like a life in Peace for sure.

We can't keep turning down the soft gentle nudges at our heart by the Holy Spirit. We need to wake up and be as consistent as possible in the ways of our God! Remember our bodies belong to God it is His temple within us this is where we can find Him thru the works of His Holy Spirit; we need to be in-retrospect, harmonized in praise and song so that we can be openly minded of His ways, they are better than our ways. Let me say this in closing this sovereign step of the Holy Spirit; Matthew 10-32, the Spirit guides us to say "Whoever acknowledges me before others, I will also acknowledge him before my Father in heaven".

4

HEAVENLY SPIRIT OF GOD

d.   Do you remember the Gifts and the Fruits of the Holy Spirit; I believe they are what God wrote on our hearts for us to lead a good life as Christ has showed us to do.

The Gifts we receive are God's perception of our human needs! The Holy Spirit determines how we get to use them? When we associate with other Christians we actually can help each other to find the gifts that we need to sustain the whole body of Christ. As Jesus put it the loaf of bread represented His body, when He blessed the bread and broke the bread He was sharing His body with all of us. Each person has many parts of his body to represent himself, I.E. the head bone is connected to the shoulder bone, the shoulder bone is connected to the arm bone, and all of our human bones are connected to each other to form one body! The Church of God is also that way, all of us have gifts and when we work them with respect, and then the Church can become a more stable place.

A very dear friend of mine Pastor Ted Hulbert wrote in his book "Romance with Romans"; that the first part of Romans is what God did for us, and the last part was what we may do for God thru the work of the Holy Spirit!

We must take the work of the Holy Spirit very convincingly as He comes to us in a new birth way thru our baptism. In (John 3:5-6) we find the message of "Born of the Spirit." We cannot enter the kingdom of God unless we are born of the water and of the Spirit? When I look at my baptism I was washed in the water and as I came up out of the water I asked God the Father to give to me the Holy Spirit to guide me in all those things that Almighty God wrote on my heart. I who was born of the flesh am now born of the Spirit!

We must rely on our Faith in order for the Holy Spirit to work in us, not everyone believes that the things Jesus did are true, so they become weak and the Grace of God who gives us all things especially Faith falls apart. The Holy Spirit does not give us Faith but He enables us to use every bit of our believing is true. Remember this when we are submerged in the water we die as Christ did, we rise to lead a new life and are led by the Spirit and He makes quick haste for us to believe in all things we have faith in. We believe this Jesus was born of the flesh in the womb of a virgin, He died on the cross for our sins; and He was resurrected on the third day and He ascended to God the Father and sits at His right hand. Without the Holy Spirit convicting us on these things we neither would believe nor would our faith be established. It is the work of God the Holy Spirit that we are able to believe as He comes to us when we ask for Him in our Spiritual baptism!

I started out talking of the Gifts and the Fruits of the Holy Spirit; without the fruits we would not be able to understand the Gifts. Each one has nine (9) parts, without the fruits of Love, Joy, Peace, Patience, Gentleness, Goodness, Kindness Faithfulness, and of course Self Control; we would not be able to use or understand the Gifts of the Spirit. In looking at the gift of wisdom, we need love to understand that. Knowledge brings us joy in our lives. Then with faith we can have a peace within ourselves one that surpasses the amount of a mustard seed. With healing we must have patience as our time and Gods time are very different. Then there is the working of miracles as Jesus should compassion for those He healed it was thru His kindness they were given to being healed. It is thru prophecy that the virtues of goodness showing us decency and the righteousness of a good man's values. The discerning spirits can be detected but we must build up a faithfulness of the Holy Trinity, for it is the acts of the Spirit that will give us the gift to discerning. Then there is the gift of tongues and the gift to interpret them. These gifts are not so beautiful than we can discern, and not everyone can talk in tongues, nor should they if they cannot interpret this heavenly language. We see that a special gentleness of the spoken tongues. Then we see that self-control is needed in order to have it interpreted.

We must remember to acquire the fruits of the Spirit first before we seek wisdom and knowledge and the rest of the gifts give to us thru God and the Spirit will guide us in all things of our almighty God.

5

SPIRIT ACTING FOR JESUS

e.   The New Testament word is all about Jesus and His mission here on Earth! The word is of His Birth, Ministry, Death, and His Resurrection. Some don't understand the position of the Holy Spirit or how He fits in?

The work of the Holy Spirit as Jesus is outlined in John 15: 26-27, and in all of John 16: The Spirit is the advocate of the truth from the Father, and He will testify of all those things Jesus has done; as you should testify of the things you believe in. The Apostles actually saw firsthand all the marvels of Jesus, you and I must use the Grace of Faith and all that is written and what they have seen is true. This is the time to invoke Hebrews 11-1 Faith is the belief of those things hoped fore are true, and the assurance of those things we are not able to see. We are to be encouraged by this statement for it surely preserves our Faith.

In Hebrews Chapter 11, we see the examples of Faithfull men, the first is Enoch he was so righteous in Gods eyes he was taken up to heaven at Gods command he did not die he was taken up! Then there was Abraham, he was told that he would be the father of many nations, at age 75, it took 25 more years before he had a direct descendant; this was at the ripe old age of 100 years old and his wife well past child bearing age at 90. They both had faith that God would provide. We can continue with many more examples of Faith like Noah, and Moses, they too showed great faith; "without faith it is impossible to please God", Hebrews 11-6. Why is that so because Hebrews tells us this "anyone who calls upon God must actually believe He exists"? It is thru the Holy Spirit that causes us too earnestly to seek God in all matters!

Jesus did give us another helper and He will be with us forever, even to the full Spirit of truth. God's Grace came to us as Jesus was preparing to ascend to heaven. This Spirit was not like the Spirit of America or the Spirit of St. Louis. The Holy Spirit given to us by the request of Jesus thru the Father; this brings us a freedom and liberty of another kind? In our Baptismal promises we see the following, faith, assurance, consolation and a forgiveness that can come only thru the Holy Spirit.

The Spirit acts for God and Jesus as an advocate and a counselor and He will provide grace and peace whenever we need it. Our Lord Jesus knew that there would be days that we would not be able to cope with; it would then be the Spirits encouragement that would keep us going. The Holy Spirit is and will always be the greatest servant of God and there is no reason why He cannot be the servant of Jesus to deliver and guide any and all messages thru our inner being which the heart is the storage place of everything God wants us to know.

In Jude 19, it tells us that if you do not have a spirit then one is considered not saved. Are you willing to leave this world with-out knowing where you are going? In Hebrews 11-8, Abraham knew not where he was going or what he would do; but his faith in Gods judgment made him a righteous man. Abraham was told there would be a great reward for him, and we are also told of the riches of believing in all that Jesus has told us! If you died today or tomorrow do you know what lies ahead for you. The Holy Spirit will convict you of all things of God be prepared to lead a life of faith and righteousness, and your reward of heaven will be guaranteed.

6

HIS INDWELLING WITHIN OUR HEART.

f.   The Holy Spirit of God does Indwell with in our Hearts! (Ephesians 1:11-14) God has predestined each of us who will receive the Holy Spirit and who accept that Jesus the Christ is the Son of God. In other words we have a guarantee once we receive the Spirit, we have Him forever. (John 14:16)

I have heard about Pastors that preach that once you have received the spiritual gift and its purpose is fulfilled, it will cease. How can faith cease or wisdom or knowledge or any of the gifts of the Spirit for that matter? When we die I suppose? We will no longer need the body we are in and any and all of its parts, including the brain; for we will inherit a new body and it will be a spiritual one!

If anyone does not have the Spirit of Christ, he does not belong to Christ! (Romans 8:9) How can anyone believe that they will lose the

Holy Spirit, in John 3-16? "God so loved the world that He gave His one and only Son, whoever believes in Him Shall not perishes but have everlasting life." God made us a promises and it is for all eternity.

We can go back in this book and find that we have stated that some people have found difficulty in understanding that the Holy Spirit is actually a person like, the Father and Jesus as they are a part of the Holy Trinity? He cannot be touched or seen yet He is there for you and me. He does dwell in us and every time we need Him we call upon Him and He is right there for us! He is called our helper and if you think about it this title can be only assigned to an actual person that does want to help us?

Jesus said in John 14:16 "I shall ask the Father to send you a comforter (helper) and He will be with you forever!"

The understanding of the Indwelling of the Holy Spirit started with Jesus going into the desert for forty days and forty nights? In Matthew 4:1, "Jesus was led by the Holy Spirit into the desert." Of course we know that He was tempted by Satan three different times. Jesus came out of the desert triumphantly!

We can be the walking spiritual image of God (Genesis 1:27) as we were created in their image; (The Father, Son and the Spirit). We should think of ourselves as a walking practical dictionary!

We get to inform others of the promises that Jesus made to us that God would send His Spirit to each of us as we called upon Him to be indwelled with us in our hearts! His promises did not come without a commitment? In John 14:21 Jesus said "obey the commands I have given you." We cannot separate the love of the Father or the loving of one another. Obedience to the Laws of God is paramount! Jesus promised us an advocate of the truth, a counselor, comforter, helper, and a redeemer and that He would indwell in us and He would intercede for us, to God the Father Almighty!

Jesus knew He would be leaving this world, and He wanted not only the Disciples of the first century, but you and I the new disciples of Jesus to receive the Gift of God!

This gift is available to all who believe that Jesus is the Son of God, and He will indwell in each of us who call upon Him!

7

AS THE MOLDER

g. The Holy Spirit as the molder is accomplished by what I like to use (in songs) the first song is; "Spirit of the living God fall fresh on me, melt me, mold me, make me and use me", for what- ever God has predestined me to be or do in this life. Then there is the song, "This is the day that the Lord hath made", we should rejoice and be glad in it, for he has indwelled in me for a molding like that of clay. Then there is the song of welcome as we ask Him this, "Spirit of God descends, upon my Heart". He is to take all earthly things from it and place me in a spirit of thanksgiving, by taking all my weaknesses away and put my heart in a teaching mode of answered prayer.

There will come with the indwelling a challenge, one of can I really do all this that is required of me? Do I have a relationship with My Lord and savior? Do I believe wholly in the risen lord Jesus the Christ? Do I know the power of His indwelling Spirit?

We have some questions to answer, but the Lord Jesus said to His disciple and to us, (Matthew 28:18) "All power has been given to me therefore go and make disciples of all nations". Everyone is included in this command of Christ!

There is a Justification by Faith found in Romans 5:10, (Paraphrased); "once we were enemies of God and now being reconciled to God Almighty, because of the death of His Son, we shall be saved by His life, and the promise of the Gift of God that Jesus asked for(that of the Holy Spirit) to fall fresh on us! It is not by believing, nor that of repentance but that of Faith of those things we do not see?

In Genesis 1, God looked upon the Earth that was form-less and without shape He had the Holy Spirit perform a molding at that time. God's greatest servant did in fact mold the earth as God directed! He arranged the stars, the planets, their moons and all of the constellations so that mankind could navigate on land, the sea and in the air! That was a molding for the begging of all mankind. The Holy Spirit rearranged the earth so that the mountains would appear and capture the water that would be needed to satisfy the growth of all green things like plants and the forest that would give mankind the oxygen to breath. As all of this happened, mankind figured out how to prove God did create all things that matter. The law of "A Bio-Genesis" was formed stating that, we needed five rules to prove that it was God that indeed create the Heavens and the Earth! There had to be a TIME frame to be approved that was the Beginning, then what was the FORCE, that would be GOD Himself, then what was the ACTION, that would be HE CREATED, then came the use of SPACE, as we see it is all of the HEAVENS, and finally, the MATTER that was used would be the Earth itself. "Time, Force, Action. Space, and Matter the five fundamentals of the "A-Bio-Genesis Law". This proves the words of Genesis 1; ("In the Beginning God Created the Heavens and the Earth.") Ten of the most beautiful words mankind could ever read!

Jesus came that we should receive the Word of God and when Jesus left this earth He promised us the Gift of God, that being the Third person of the Holy Trinity, The Holy Spirit of God; He would guide us by indwelling in us and molding us to what God had pre-destined us to be "Amen".

CHAPTER 3   SUMMARY

The Third Step of the Holy Spirit is our use of the Power of the Holy Spirit!

1. Where did His power come from? First of all it is thru our Faith that we believe that He actually exists? There were three questions we asked and we answered them by selecting three righteous

persons of the Bible! The first was Miriam sister of Moses, she was an anointed one of the Spirit of God and known as a Prophetess and she taught the women of Israel in song and dance, she was a blessing to Moses until she became jealous of him and she wanted more recognition! She was struck with a plague but she was healed after Moses prayed for her, but she died shortly after the healing. It was her repenting and faith in Moses prayer that she was healed.

The next one who also was anointed one of the Spirit of God was Samson! He belonged to the Nazarenes and they grew hair without cutting it. Samson and all others believed that it was his hair that gave him great strength, (that was not really proven in the Bible?)

Samson with a women named Delilah and she was hired to get the source of his strength it took several trials before Samson gave in and his thinking that it was his hair cost him all his strength. His eyes were gouged out and they used him as a slave. Samson also repented and promised God one last time he would destroy the temple of the Philistines and the Philistine people! The Spirit of God came upon him and he accomplished what he promised and also died doing it.

The third person I used was Jepthah; he became King and did well in the eyes of the Lord. After a while he came into his own way of doing things. He did not do well unto all the people and his brother ran him out of Israel. Israel was about to be attacked by a country that Jepthah had beaten in the past; his brother could not stop them and went to find Jepthah to help Israel. Jepthah agreed if they would grant him to be King once again.

They agreed and he said that if the Spirit of God would lead him to a victory he would sacrifice the first virgin that greeted him after his home coming. This turned out to be his only daughter. Jepthah did what he had promised to the Spirit of God and to the people.

2 The second way of the Spirit is how He caters to our every need. This is found in three concerns in the use of Courage, Patience and that of

a Peace in us. I have found that praying in the time of fear will build up my strength and the lasting effect is courage. When we pray to the Spirit we pray with love and understanding; that gives us access to our own built in courage!

Patience on the other hand is one of being quiet and listening for the response of the Spirit within us! Remember this Holy Spirit, is in you, and all things of God the Father and those of Jesus can be recalled to assist us in our needs of courage and patience and an inner peace. I mentioned a (Trust and Obey) syndrome; for thirty days we were actually making the verse in James 1:25 become visible (trust is) all about one looking intently into God's perfect laws that gives each of us freedom and anyone who continues to do this each day, he should not forget what he has heard, but obeying it as well is blessed in what he does. We should remember this that the Holy Spirit builds us up to receive the courage we look for and the patience to wait for it that gives us a peace that comes from Jesus; and the Holy Spirit confirms it. We will receive the fruits of the Spirit in a same manner, like love, joy, peace, patience, goodness, gentleness, kindness, faithfulness, and at last but of course not less than the other is self-control! (Galatians 5:27)

3. His Sovereignty is in the fact that he reigns with all truth in all matters. We are to obey what he puts in our hearts. Because He will never lead us into trouble or let us go astray, we must believe in Him. When we talked about the wind that we fell and hear, this is the Holy Spirit we can't see Him but we can feel Him in our hearts?

Jesus has been given all the power in heaven and on earth to make us all disciples to go forth to preach and teach the word of God. The Holy Spirit will anoint each one who carries this spirit of love for one another! We must remember that it is the soft gentle nudges that the Holy Spirit is giving to our hearts to remind us that our bodies are the temple of God.

The Holy Spirit guides us to acknowledge Him before others as He will do so for us to God the Father.

4.	The heavenly Spirit of God gives us all gifts, and the fruits of His Spirit; I believe that God wrote them all on our hearts and each one (9) nine of each complement each other. Without the fruits we would not be able to understand the gifts? I used some examples like Wisdom without Love we cannot understand it! Then there is Knowledge it brings us a Joy in our hearts and mind! In mankind there is the decency to do well unto all of mankind for we pass this way once in our lives! To understand the Fruits of the Spirit first in our lives it then makes it easier to receive the gifts of the Spirit!

5.	The mission of Jesus has been put in our hearts for us to recall His deeds here on earth. We have access to them through the Holy Spirit, for the Spirit will act as Jesus to us thru our Faith in those things of God can be recalled for our daily use! The Holy Spirit is our helper and He will be with us all our lives all we have to do is call upon Him any time we need help! He therefore acts as Jesus in our lives! Remember without faith it is impossible to please God.

6.	For the indwelling of the Holy Spirit in our hearts we must actually believe He exist as stated in Hebrews 11-6. You and I get to act like the disciples of the 1st Century we have been empowered to teach others of Jesus the Son of God. When Jesus promised us the Holy Spirit of God it did not come without a commitment. As stated in John 14:21, Jesus said, "obey my commands I give you, the love of the Father cannot be separated from loving one another. "We can receive the Holy Spirit at baptism just ask, and you will receive!

7.	What better way is there for the Holy Spirit to can mold us? He melts us down as thru baptism, when we come up out of the water we are cleansed from sin as being buried with Christ, and we start a new life in Jesus. This is done thru the help of the Spirit of God. He then indwells with us upon your command of asking God for Him to enter into your life. Remember this Jesus would ask God to send us the Holy Spirit it then became the Promises of God for all who would ask for Him!

VISUALIZING - HIM:

THE FOURTH OF SEVEN STEPS

Chapter 4

─────❧─────

Holy Spirit Seen as Visual Symbol.

The next Seven Ways are those of the Visual Symbols and the signs that I felt would give us some benefit in visualizing the Holy Spirit. The key here is (seen) as actually visualizing what the Holy Spirit is all about! Not actually seeing Him but the feeling of His presence within our hearts, our minds and our consciousness will give us a view of Him. We are expected to follow a path laid out for us, by our Lord Jesus; we need to submit to the Spirit as we would Jesus!

I believe that the Holy Spirit is the protector of mankind's (Free -Will), Jesus in John 14-16 assured us that we would be protected, comforted and He would send us the Spirit of Truth! He is to be with us until Jesus returns and gathers us up to be with Him in His Father's house.

How does this help us in deciding how to worship God? Mankind's free-will is extremely tricky; we are able to do whatever we want but there are consequences for all our actions!

Jesus tells us in John 14-6 that He is, "the way, the truth and the life; no one comes unto the father unless it is by me (Jesus)". When we call upon the Holy Spirit He reminds us of our responsibilities? Now if your goal in life is not to live in heaven with the peace and serenity of the Heavenly Father; continue doing whatever you want. However if you do as the Holy Spirit directs you, to obey Jesus' every command, His every word, and follow His path which is laid out for you and seek to help others in search of Christ Jesus! If we obey the will of God thru the Holy Spirit we can expect to visualize Him with us in a room in our Fathers mansion.

a.   We will first look at the visual symbol of the Dove of Peace. It is the most famous one I found in the Bible! The Dove was given to us at the Baptism of our Lord Jesus in Matthew 3-16. I have used it on the cover of this book and to emphasize the fire of the Holy Spirit at Pentecost! The Spirit as the Dove came on Jesus and He stayed with Jesus right into the desert where He was confronted by Satan three times and Jesus came up victories. The Dove was used as a peace offering by the Israelites; Mary and Joseph were so poor this is what was available to them when they presented Jesus at the Temple.

b.   In the military the Sergeant would select the strongest and most reliable man to lead the way; it was called take the Point! God has always sent the Holy Spirit to take the Point to guide and counsel all those that He has selected to receive His Spirit! We will now compare the Strength of the Spirit as we have seen them in the use of the elements. This time we see His strength come to those who use Faith, as their sole support for the Spirit in our everyday needs. Mankind cannot see the Holy Spirit as he is depicted in the Bible! Mankind was able to see Jesus, but not God or His Spirit, for that matter! The Bible does give us pictures of what the Spirit represents; we just have to visualize them in our minds and then associate with what is written in our hearts those things He wants us to know and what He is trying to get across to us!

c.   Now let us look at Love, it is an attention getter for sure; God does all things in Love! I.e. God uses the Holy Spirit in putting people together. There is a beautiful story that is in two parts that leads to the throne of David and to Christ Himself! We recognize the fact that God has written everything we need to know on our hearts! Our actions whether good or bad call attention to how we could have had the Spirit lead us? If, we call upon the Spirit in all matters first of all, we can have an outcome with much more desirable results! We must the gift of Love as a talent and an ability in order to share with one another.

d. Poured out like water? It was in the Old Testament that we find God poured out to those persons He chose to receive the Holy Spirit! In Exodus 31:3 "I have filled him with the Spirit of God"; this was given to Bezalel of Judah. God had just told Moses that he was to be filled with great wisdom and abilities in order for him to construct the building of the Holy Tabernacle of God! Remember when Jesus rose up from out of the water, the Spirit of God in the form of the Dove lighted upon Him. So too the Spirit came upon a man that had a talent for building; but not to the preciseness that God required. The Holy Spirit cane to fill his mind with the extra wisdom needed?

e. Everyone wants to hear the Sanctifying words that will set us all free? It can be done thru the sanctifying words of the Holy Spirit that we can go forth with our lives believing in Jesus and of all His works and words are true. It is by the grace of God that we are set apart from others to do His calling; we in turn will Glorify God as Jesus did with all that He did by obeying the Fathers word! He alone fills us with the Holy Spirit of life that we can lead a clean, fruitful one.

f. Just what is it that we can see in the Seven-lamps or the seven lamp stands? Lamps were used in the Old Testament to light a path way or the inside of a home! When the Tabernacle was built there was a single Lamp stand with seven holders; this was the source of light when the Priest was praying to God. The Spirit gives us ways to make our light shine. We hope to see that the Holy Spirit is our light when we also talk to God! There is a story in Matthew 25-1-13, "The Parable of the Ten Virgins", we will look at?

g. Visualizing what happened at Pentecost I feel gives us the greatest of all visions that can express how we can see and feel the Holy Spirit! Next to the Dove appearing on the shoulder of Jesus at His Baptism, would be the day the Holy Spirit came to the Twelve Apostles and the hundreds of disciples in the upper room! He appeared on the heads of all who were there. It was astonishing to read how all this appeared to all who saw it happened? Pentecost is an event that we all need to look at more closely. To visualize the Spirit as flames bouncing off your head when the spirit comes on to you, has to be a feeling that ignites your spirit to be joined with Gods Holy Spirit?

1

AS THE DOVE

a. The appearance of the Dove in three of the Gospels (Matthew, Mark, Luke) Give about the same accounting and description of the Holy Spirit as the Dove from above! The Spirit descended upon Him thus anointing Him that Jesus would begin His ministry at about thirty years of age. The Dove does symbolize the gentleness and purity of His character, but we find that when He descended from the sky that was all clouded up; thunder and lightning was seen and heard as the voice of God spoke His words, "this is my Son, whom I love, and with Him I am well pleased". What a day the Lord hath made let us rejoice and be glad in it.

The appearance of the Holy Spirit as the Dove marks the occasion of the Holy Trinity; the voice of Father as God, Jesus as the Son of God standing in the water, and the Dove as the Holy Spirit, all present at the same time; and they are involved with the baptism of our Lord Jesus. Now Jesus at thirty years of age is stepping out into the world to start his mission that the Father had sent him there to do! The Spirit will lead Him into the desert to face Satan and his challengers. Wouldn't it be nice to know that the Spirit as the Dove actually flew along and guided Him? We know that He was full of the Spirit as He confronted the trials that the Devil put Him through! He immerged from the desert of trials victorious. There should be no guess work in figuring out who the Holy Spirit was and is in any part of the New Testament? This showing of the Holy Trinity as the Dove at this time was for John the Baptist and his mission. Can you imagine the people there watching in complete awe?

When John the Baptist was finished with each person he would tell them this, "I baptize you with water unto repentance but there will come one who is mightier than me and He shall baptize you with the Holy Spirit." This is the same Spirit that appeared as the Dove from above! (Matthew 3-11) `

I look at Genesis 1:2b as saying "now the Dove (Holy Spirit of God was moving over the top of the waters" I like visualizations and when I can see the Spirit hovering, moving or breathing life into us on any situation that we may ask help for; I see Him as the Dove flying around and being over us at all times waiting for us to ask of Him our hearts desires. The Holy Spirit was able to do certain things in the early era of the Church! Look at 1Peter 1:10-12, He was a part of the telling of the future, and He brought the word of God to the minds of Preachers and Teachers who taught and wrote of the future.

The Holy Spirit as the Dove in my visualization did many things as He was with Christ on this earth? He was very helpful in Jesus completing His mission on earth! God gave to Jesus all of His Spirit! (Luke 1:35) He was the one who taught men to understand as Jesus was teaching to them! (John 14:25-26)

"The Holy Spirit actually raised Jesus from the Dead", and this Dove of vision the same Holy Spirit does live in our Hearts and in our minds! (Romans 8-11)

Do you remember the presentation of Jesus at the Temple? Found in Luke 2:23-24 every first-born was offered unto God, and they had to make a sacrifice in the form of, "a pair of Doves or two pigeons". This is because they were so poor they couldn't offer up a lamb to be sacrificed! This was all done IAW Numbers 3:11-13.

The visualization of the Spirit as a pure white Dove is wonderful; but remember this He is a part of the Holy Trinity the three persons in one God; He is as real as a person and is alive in us today and will always be with us, as He came into Christ when He became flesh. He is special and has done many special things in my life.

2

AS STRENGTH

b.   Comparing the Strengths of the Spirit with a person from the Bible I can think of Sampson (Judges 13:1-25). The examples of his strength that were given to us came to him from the Holy Spirit. God was using Sampson to show the power of God's strength over all matters that needed examples made of!

I am writing this during the month of December and I can't help comparing Sampson's birth to that of the Virgin birth of our Lord Jesus! There was a man named Manoah his wife was unable to bear children. One day an Angel of God appeared to her and said; "I know that you are sterile and childless and cannot bear children; (but) you will give birth to a son".

The Angel also gave instructions of how she was to care for herself and for the child. The woman told her husband, he prayed over the matter that they would get more instructions on how she should take care of her body and how they should raise this child that God wants them to have.

These instructions were those of how to raise a child of a Nazirite's! She should not eat any unclean foods, drink wine or any fermented fluids! Their son is never to have his head shaved and he will be set apart for God and raised as a Nazirite's! This is found in Numbers (6-1) a vow of consecration to God of his or her life for a specific time period. The wife of Manoah gave birth to a son and he was named Sampson. This child received the Holy Spirit while he was still in the mother's womb; sound familiar?

In the story of Sampson we find a negative and a positive view of his life? By this I mean that it would appear that Sampson sounded like some up start up kid showing off his muscles more than one who was filled with the Holy Spirit of God. His strength was due to the fact that the Spirit was his source of power. When we look at some of the antics he performed they were not what Mr. Spock would call logical?

In chapter 14 of Judges we see the story of Sampson traveling with his parents to Timnah in Palestine to find a bride for him! On the way a lion jumped out behind his parents but in his path and he ripped the lions jaw apart like a young goat. He then threw the carcass to the side of the road! His parents did not see what he did. They continued on to the village? He selected his wife and returned home. Sometime later in returning on the same road to marry his wife, he felt the need for something sweet and remembered the lions carcass and saw that a bee hive was established in it so he dipped his hand in it and brought forth some honey and was eating it and offered some to his parents, but he did not again tell them where he got it from! What he did here was against the Nazirite's vow (Numbers 66-7), but it was what the Holy Spirit wanted him to do! We have to remember this that God was looking to punish the Palestinians and he was using Sampson thru the Holy Spirit's power in Sampson to accomplish this! For instance the reasoning of taking on as his wife a woman from Palestine doesn't make sense unless you put God in the equation! God was going to get at the Palestinians one way or the other, and Power of Sampson filled with the Spirit was God's way! I have read that someone once compared Superman and Sampson they both had a weakness as you and I would also have; there was the Kryptonite that was not good for Superman, and for Sampson it was beautiful and sexy women! When we look ahead in time we can expect the Church to be seduced by the religions of the future accepting and bowing down to the establishment of the time. Churches will compromise their values of Jesus and of Gods tolerance of what the truth is. As seen in the Book of Revelations! Our strength lies in only one person, Jesus; the Holy Spirit of God.

3

AS LOVE

c.   The greatest love stories ever told I found in the Bible! As a matter of fact there were many love stories. I would like to focus on two of them. These stories began about the same time? Care to guess!!!!

If you thought of Naomi and Ruth, Boaz and Ruth! The Holy Spirit has influenced each of these examples of love that are used .Love should feel like a natural thing for us; we were made in God's image and "God first loved us" as show in 1 John 4-19 It is said that all love comes from God we don't generate it He feeds it to us threw His Spiritual gifts!

Naomi left Israel with her husband and sons during a time of famine. This was not the best of times for her for she lost her husband and sons. She had two Daughters in law to care for so out of love she told them to go back to their families that she released them from any responsibilities to her!(Book of Ruth 1:8-15) One left begrudgingly, the other refused to leave her by herself and proclaimed that she Naomi was the only family she had (Ruth 1: 16-18). Ruth made a convincing story to Naomi, "I will go where ever you go, your people will be my people and your God will be my God". This is so powerful, and so full of love that Naomi stopped trying to convict her to leave! This expression of loyalty and loving devotion of Ruth to Naomi, gives us a look at Ruth's character. Her commitment to Naomi puts her in the same situation as Naomi but she is willing to share her life with her mother-in-law! Together they are willing to face any obstacles that they will come across when they arrive in Bethlehem. Now Naomi was very bitter and felt God had punished her by taking her husband and two sons. When she arrived in Bethlehem she told the women there not to use her name of Naomi, but instead to use Mara for the (meaning) "The Lord has made me bitter". They went to her old house and Ruth became accustomed to everyday living! Ruth would go into the field and glean for stalks of wheat!

The second love story is when Ruth meets Boaz who appears to be a rich relative of Naomi's! Ruth said to Naomi let me go and glean in the fields so we will have a source of food! It turned out she was working in a field that belonged to Boaz. Boaz happened by and noticed her in the field and said to his foreman, "who is that young girl"? The foreman told him that it was Naomi's Moab daughter-in-law. Boaz introduced himself and told her he was aware of who she was and not to glean in any other fields but his!

Now Boaz did for her more than he would do for others, and he assured her no one would lay a hand on her and she was asked to dine with him on that first day! When she arrived home Naomi was really surprised at the quantity of the wheat and barley she brought home! When Ruth told her whose field she gleaned in, then Naomi told Ruth it was her relative?

Things were going along smoothly for them, when one day Naomi said to Ruth, "we need to find you your own house that you may be cared for". Then Naomi laid out some plans for Ruth to court Boaz with the hope that he would end up marrying her!

Now nothing Naomi told Ruth would be out of line, but that it would be a loving seductive encounter? Ruth agreed with Naomi and would do everything she said! Ruth dressed in fine clothes and went at night to lie at the feet of Boaz while he was sleeping and in the middle of the night, something startled Boaz and he woke to find Ruth at his feet! Now Boaz was not a young man, so he blessed her for what kindness she was showing in not looking for one younger.

This of course according to tradition was a form of looking for a husband and Boaz acknowledges this. He told Ruth he would have to ok it with another relative who has priority over these matters. He also assured her that if he didn't want to marry her, he Boaz would honor his commitment to her!

Boaz called for an assembly of the Elders and it included the guardian redeemer of the clan of Ruth and Boaz. Now according to the Jewish Law he has sole authority to buy the land or sell the land that Naomi's husband owned. Boaz being the second in line, of guardianship of this clan; was acting out of love for all parties! He knew this man would not accept the Moabite Ruth, because it would jeopardize his family's rights of having to share yet with another family! Boaz is committed to love Ruth back for her expression of love shown to him on the threshing floor! The guardian and the Elders all agreed to the marriage and property rights for Boaz and Naomi and Ruth.

The marriage was consummated in a deep love and the Lord blessed them with a son. Naomi took the child in her hands and blessed him and thanked God for another son. They named him O'bed and he became the father of Jesse and Jesse became the father of David.

Mary and Joseph both came from the clan of David and the Lord blessed them by sending the Holy Spirit into Mary's womb and Jesus was born unto them. Now Jesus became the greatest love story that will ever be told thru time!

4

POURED OUT LIKE WATER

d. The gift of the Holy Spirit is poured out like water to all who ask for Him to come into their lives! Most believe that He comes to us in our water baptism, as we are buried with Christ in the water and before we rise up out of the water we are asked to "ask for the Holy Spirit of God to come into our lives". The Spirit of God will come to all who ask for Him to enter into their lives. One thing for sure He will not come to anyone who does not believe that Jesus is the Son of God!

When was the last time you saw a person so convicted with the Holy Spirit standing on a street corner pouring out his love of the word of God? Surely the Holy Spirit has convicted him to share with all who pass by the love of Christ Jesus? God's love is being poured out in many ways, especially to fulfill the great commission that Jesus left for us as in Matthew 28:18-20. ("Go forth and make disciples of all nations").

God's love was poured out on the whole world at Calvary; He sent His only begotten Son to die for us on the cross! In Romans 5-8 God demonstrates His love for the whole world in the fact that, "while we were still sinners He died for us".

The Law of God (Ten Commandments) hammered out with the finger of God, given to Moses was perfect, good, just and holy! The thing about the Law was not Grace but that of Sin. Once you break one of the Commands of God you break all of them. Jesus came to us that we may be saved thru the Grace of God and the washing of our sins thru His Blood! Jesus was the sacrificial Lamb of God! Jesus promised us that the Holy Spirit would come to us and he would convict us of all truth in all matters?

In the Book of Genesis, God Poured out his Spirit upon the Earth. The Spirit of God is the greatest servant of God! He did everything God asked Him to do. Then God breathe into man and created Adam! This was the last act of God using His Spirit; the use of the Spirit became the Holy Spirit of God in all other matters. The Holy Spirit became a Judge, informer, and lived in the hearts of men to convict them of the true ways that God wanted them to perform!

The use of water is often associated with the Holy Spirit? In Ezekiel 47:1-12 we find the Spirit leading Ezekiel on a tour of the Temple; this can be considered as a transforming stream of water coming from the throne of God and getting deeper as it travels and the farther it travels the more of a restoration it will bring. This river matches I think the one found in Revelations 22. This would be called the river of life showing us visions of our hopes and dreams of eternal life. God's presence produces what we would need. The trees in both visions are those that would provide sustenance; and the further it travels in both visions it restores the land. All of these visions given to Ezekiel and the John show us that all our hopes will be fulfilled and God will be the temple for us to Worship. I believe that in Heaven the universal language will be our Faith. "Joy is the end results of your Faith and the satisfaction of your Salvation". (1Peter 8-9)

The ancient Israelites based their hopes on a Temple were in Revelations we won't need a Temple we will have God and we will see Him with our new spiritual bodies.

In Revelations 22-17 says, "The Spirit and the Bride say "Come", and let the one who hears say, "Come"! Let the one who is thirsty come and let the one who wishes, take the free gift of the water of life.

5

HIS WORD

e. "Oh come Holy Spirit of God"; that's exactly what happened on the day of Pentecost! The Holy Spirit was given to twelve men on that day and it was a site to behold! He came that they would be able to go out into the world and preach the Gospel of the word of God as Jesus told it to them. It was by the grace of God that these men and many others in that upper room were given the Holy Spirit. Given so that they may go forth and give the word and they would make changes in the hearts and minds of men and women. They would convict the sinners to be saints and the unbelievers to be faithful followers of the word of God! It is the promise of Jesus that the Spirit delivers to fulfill Christ message to all of those who will believe in the Son of God. The Spirit will set them on fire to receive Christ love. There will be great joy and rejoicing and thanks of God that the Spirit is received in Jesus' name. (Acts 2-4) Tells us, "and they were filled with the Holy Spirit and began to speak in other tongues as the Spirit gave to them an utterance of languages".

When Jesus entered into the desert He was accompanied by the Holy Spirit where He was tempted with trials by Satan? Matthew 4-4 says, but He answered to Satan, "It is written, Man shall not live by bread alone, but by every word that comes from the mouth of God."

You remember the story, for forty days and nights Jesus wandered in the wilderness without food, water or sleep! Jesus full of the Spirit of God kept Satan at bay because of the Word of God! God filled Jesus in a supernatural way with the Spirit. So to can you be filled with the

Spirit for your nourishment! Jesus relied on the Spirit of God not His own miraculous Powers, in order to survive this ordeal.

There are some verses in the sanctifying Words of the Gospel; that I would love to give to you in helping your visual quest of the Holy Spirit.

Proverbs 16-9, "the heart of a man plans his way, but the Spirit of the Lord establishes his steps".

Joshua 24-15, "and if it is evil in your eyes to serve the Lord, chose this day whom you will serve,(if you chose to serve other gods instead of our Lord take head); But as for me and my house I will serve my Lord".

John 7-17 "If anyone's will is to do God's will he will know the teaching is from God or whether I am speaking of my own authority".

Galatians 5:16-17, "but I say walk by the Spirit, and you will not gratify the desires of the flesh. For the desires of the flesh are against the Spirit, and the desires of the Spirit are against the flesh, for these are opposed to each other, to keep you from doing the things you want to do".

It is the sanctifying Words of God that set us free to do His will and carry on the work of Jesus. We enhance our lives by believing that the works and miracles of Jesus are so very true. It is by the grace of God that we are set apart to do His calling; He alone fills us with the Holy Spirit of a life that we need to lead in order for us to be more fruitful.

We as children of God, rely on the strength of the Spirit and the forgiving grace of Christ our Lord!

The word of God sustains us through the trails and temptations of this life. The word of God defends us against the Devil and all his lies! We are thankful to God for giving to us His words that will nourish and sustain us in the way, truth and the life we will lead on this earth. In Acts 1-8, "you will receive power when the Holy Spirit comes upon you, and you will be my witnesses in Jerusalem and in all Judea and Samaria, and to, the ends of the earth".

6

SEVEN LAMPS

f. (1) An Unlit Lamp indicates a lack of vision? (2)The wise ones took oil in jars? (3) There is a light that shines in the darkness. (4) The darkness is not understood? (5)Your word is like a lamp unto my feet? (6)The Ten Commandments are a lamp for our ways? (7)There is coming a day when a lamp will not be needed?

In the story of the ten virgins (Matthew 25) all ten of them took a lamp, but only five took extra oil in a jar! In this story we find that we need to be prepared at all times.

The Holy Spirit provides us with enough information to keep any lamp lit. In Him there is life and that life is in us and He is the light of all those who accept Jesus as the Son of God. We must be prepared to use the light of the Holy Spirit in sharing the Good News of Jesus with others; we can't wait until we see Jesus coming on a cloud! The five virgins that were running out of oil for their lamps asked the other five to give them some oil; they said no! If we give you our oil we may not have enough to keep our lamps burning until the bridegroom returns! So they went looking to buy oil and guess what the bridegroom came. Keeping watch for the second coming of Christ is of the essence, but no one knows the hour of the day so be prepared? Being prepared cannot be a shared responsibility or even one to be transferred to someone else! The Spirit in you is responsible to you so that you can share the word of God with others but you can't force them to accept being prepared?

MY HOLY SPIRIT

We who believe in one God, shows us there are three different persons in Him. They are all equal in nature to God because they are God; God the Father, God the Son, and God as the Holy Spirit. We need to keep in prayer that the Holy Spirit empowers us and keeps us safe from the many different enticements that this world imposes on us.

God imposes all things to us through His Holy Spirit! Jesus is God and the Holy Spirit is God; we may not be able to see them but they are working in us at all times, we just have to call upon them to visualize they are present! I heard Billy Graham say we should not call the Holy Spirit an (it) but we should refer to Him as a (HE)!

The Holy Spirit enforces all that Jesus represents all of His teaching and reminders of all of His miracles. God sent Jesus to express the will of God to all that would believe in Him.

When we are exposed to the Holy Spirit because we are known to come from the Darkness into the Light? (Colossians 1:13-14) tells us, "God has delivered us from the domain of the darkness and transferred us to the kingdom of His beloved Son, in whom we have redemption, and the forgiveness of sins"! Our lives at times, were full of turmoil, chaos and deception. This is because we were born into darkness and into sin? There is a price to be paid for sin; and that is death! We have been rescued by the Holy Spirit in the fact that He reminds us of all the teaching of our Lord Jesus. We have been redeemed by the blood of Jesus and the Spirit holds the blood over us like in a jar and washes us and anointing us to be cleansed as we call upon Him asking for forgiveness. All of this brings us into a state of reconciliation to God the Father; we are then saved because of the blood of Jesus and the acceptance of our baptism of the water and of receiving of the Holy Spirit of God! God then will see us as blameless, pure and even spotless, for we have been washed white as snow in the blood of Jesus!

We realize that as sinners we have died with Christ our Lord on the cross and that because of Him, our sins no longer define us and they cannot destroy us. It is by our Faith that we ask for the Holy Spirit to recall all things that grant us a peace in the newness of His life and resurrection.

The Holy Spirit will remind us it was Jesus's life given for our lives and the destiny He chose is to be our destiny by faith for all of us right now! God has given us the Holy Spirit so that we may discover what His will is! His Spirit talks to our spirit and tells us we are God's children, and we will always be His! Let your light shine.

Proverbs 6-23 tells us, "for this command is a lamp, this teaching is a light, and correction and instruction are the way to life." When we look at a person who hates discipline they must love death?

The Holy Spirit guides us in all matters; if we don't listen to Him we are not paying attention to the word of God! We tend to group about in darkness (Psalms 119-105). The light of a lamp is like God's word, "is like a lamp for my feet, and a light on to my path".(Ps 19-8) The precepts of the Lord are right they give way to listening, and visualizing the ways the Spirit of God wants us to see!

Here is a question, how far ahead can you see? Some say we can spot a candle light up to two or more miles away! Seriously, we generally will need a lamp to light our path! Even with a lamp we are confined to what is in front of the light? (Like-duh- man we need to be with them; they are having fun) Doing what others do and following their lead, is a typical way most teenagers follow? Teenagers are not the only ones to think that way. Proverbs 6-23 says commands are a lamp and the teaching is the light! Question what does the light show you?

The correct answer would be 'the way to life'; is keeping all the commandments the way to life? We found out with the Israelites that it was not an easy thing to do, break one command and you break them all? In Matthew 22-37-39 Jesus answered a question about the greatest commandment? He replied, "Love the Lord your God with all your heart (your whole being) and with your soul (strength) and with all your mind (thinking)", "and the second is like it: 'love your neighbor as yourself".

We as Christians are very a where that these two commands are a summary of the original Ten! (They were geared to extol the Law of Moses for more control). That is really a tough road to follow? Psalm 68:19-20 we find, "Praise is to the Lord our God and Savior, who each day bears our burdens". Jesus is God, who saves, and from Him we are able to escape from death and we see in the Holy Spirit those things that are His responsibility to make know to us as we ask for them.

7

PENTECOST

g. Pentecost is an event that I would like to look at more closely than the other visualization's. This day falls on the fiftieth day after the Sabbath of the Passover week! It is also called the Day of the Festival of Weeks. It was also known as the day that Moses received the Ten Commandments! Now this day of celebration will be known as the day that the Holy Spirit came upon the twelve Apostles, and approximately one hundred and twenty disciples that were gathered in the upper rooms! (Something similar to the upper room of the Last Supper) The Holy Spirit comes to fulfill the promises Jesus made, that the Father will send you His Holy Spirit to counsel you and comfort you and guide you in all of their and our ways in life.

We look at Acts 2:1-4 and a story will unfold? In Verse 2:2 "suddenly there was a sound like the blowing of a violent (sounding) wind that came from heaven; filling the whole house where they were sitting". In Verse 2:3 "they saw what seemed to be tongues that separated and rested on each of them." (Their heads) Fire in its self has always been associated with the deity of God?

In Exodus 3:2 Moses saw a fiery bush burning and it did not burn up with the fire; he saw an angel of the Lord there and he heard the voice of God talking to him!

In Luke 3:16 John the Baptist said, "I baptize you with water, but there is one more powerful than I who will come, the straps of whose sandals I am not worthy to untie. He will baptize you with the Holy Spirit and fire." (This was no doubt fulfilled at Pentecost) The fire of the Holy Spirit is as a cleansing power, to make things new and pure. In Hebrews 1:7, in speaking of the angels he said, "He makes His angel's Spirits and His servant's flames of fire."

We also see in Acts 2 that the Apostles were able to talk in different tongues (different languages) to all the people that were visiting in Jerusalem at this time. Now the Spirit enabled the Apostles to talk too many of the people there in their own language; the Apostles were not able to do this before and it was because of the receiving of the Holy Spirit that they could speak to the crowds that were visiting during the Festival week! They were able to declare the wonders of God to each of them; in verse 2:12 they were "Amazed and perplexed they asked of one another, what does this mean?"

It would appear that this gift of the Spirit has influenced many of these foreigners to see Jesus for the first time because of the ability of the Apostles being able to speak in their tongue (Language). Some in the crowd thought that they were drunk with wine; Peter came to their rescue with a beautiful rendition of the passages from the prophet Joel's writing. The words of Joel 2:30, "I will show wonders in the heavens and on the earth, blood and fire and billows of smoke." These events have been considered to the day of the Lord as Peter was telling, it and to the day of the Lord in the book of Revelations as I see it! When we look at the fire; this represents God's presence and that of the Holy Spirit. The blood would be that of Jesus dying for us on the cross so that His mission would be considered complete to pave the way of the Spirit!

Whenever God accepted a sacrifice in the Old Testament; He would send fire to consume it showing His approval in Spirit form!

There is only one fire that should be burning in us and that is of the Holy Spirit. Remember, the Holy Spirit did not come until the mission of Jesus was complete at Calvary! Jesus had to be crucified and raised from the dead and we had to believe in Him before we could accept the Holy Spirit of God!

Pentecost came at a price but we should give thanks for the out pouring of the Holy Spirit upon the Apostles; they preached the good news of the death of Jesus and His resurrection. This was done to reach all people of every nation in the whole world. They have caused our hearts yours and mine to be filled with the Holy Spirit.

CHAPTER 4   SUMMARY
VISIONS SEVEN WAYS

I started out this chapter with the fact that Free-Will is protected by the Holy Spirit. In Proverbs 16-9 "The heart of man plans his way, but the Lord establishes his steps". The Holy Spirit dwells within us and He is responsible to remind us of all things that are written on our hearts; therefore He is the protector of our Free-Will?

Revelations 3:20, "Behold I stand at the door and knock. If anyone hears my voice and opens the door, I will come in to him and eat with him, and he with me."

1. The Dove is a very special visualization that we looked at. It showed us the way Jesus was baptized in the water and the alighting of the dove upon his shoulder, which reminded me of the born again baptism that Jesus talked to Nicodemus about. Not that Jesus had to be born again but it was to me a reminder that we needed to look at in order to confirm what Jesus said about entering into the kingdom of God. (John 3:3-5) Jesus said, "Truly, truly I say to you unless one is born again of the water and the Spirit he cannot enter into the Kingdom of Heaven." Yes that's what I'm talking about; Jesus is filled with the Holy Spirit when He rose up, out of the water and the Dove came down from above (Heaven) and sat on His shoulder in the form of a pure white dove! To be born again is not something we do; this is considered as a gift from God!

The Holy Spirit as the Dove in my visualization did many things with Jesus who was the Messiah here on earth! God gave to Jesus all of His Spirit to be with Him in His entire time on this earth?

2. As for visualizing Him as strength I chose a human as in Sampson from the book of Judges! Sampson was of the clan of Dainties; his heroic exploits due to the strength of the Holy Spirit were of a single handed type. It would be interesting for you to compare the births of Sampson, Isaac, Ishmael, John the Baptist, and of Jesus all received a calling from the Angel of the Lord! He was born with special spiritual divine provisions about him? The birth of Sampson points out the parallels that God wants us to see. We see what God did for Israel and the actions of Sampson's are thru the Holy Spirit. Gods Spirit was one of unique powers so that he could make know that God would be the final conqueror over the Philistines! The story of Sampson is the story of Israel and God's unfailing love, and grace given to His people whom He would not desert. Sampson failed God as did Israel, but he was given a second chance, but he ended up dying; not like Israel who is still in Gods favor?

3. Everybody loves a love story, especially the one I chose with Naomi, Ruth and Boaz! This story leads us on a path straight to Jesus! These two women lost the loves of their lives and the right to have children, or more children of that marriage? There was no doubt in my mind that the Holy Spirit was in control of this story of love from the beginning of Naomi's marriage right to the Angel of The Lord talking to Mary! I realize that the greatest love story is in the greatest story ever told that of the Birth, death and ascension of our Savior Christ Jesus! When the Spirit came upon the Twelve Apostles in the upper room, He also gave birth to each of us to receive the Spirit. Acts 1:8, you will receive power when the Holy Spirit has come upon you, and you will be my witnesses; we are to witnesses unto the whole world! The time Jesus spent on earth was full of pain and suffering, and even trails? He was tested in many ways and even was subjected to Satan's powers. Jesus greatest act of love was when He died on the cross for us. His death shows us how He defeated death and His burial sanctified the graves of us all! He then rose from the grave and now sits at the right hand of

God the Father Almighty. The gift of love was given to us at the day of Pentecost; the Holy Spirit came for all of us just as Jesus said He would. The love story of Jesus is not over with; Jesus will come again just as He promised as in John 1: "where I go, you will also go." Yes that's what real love is, and we will join Him in heaven and the Holy Spirit will keep us faithful until He Jesus returns!

4. I chose being poured out like water as a visual symbol because if we are to share the word of God with others must be as fluid as water. Let it all out don't be afraid. I used the street corner evangelist as an example of spreading and sharing Gods word! The great commission of Jesus made it very clear that we should go forth and make disciples of all peoples in all nations, the whole world as Billy Graham put it. We found out at Calvary, that Gods love was poured out because Jesus died for the whole world. John 3:16 " God so loved the world that he gave His one and only Son (Jesus), that anyone who believes in Him shall not perish, but have eternal life." Remember this while we were still sinners He died for us at Calvary. In the Book of Genesis Gods greatest servant the Holy Spirit of God poured Himself over the earth, first the waters and then the mountains and then the valleys, to make sure it was right for us to live on. You and I who are filled with the Holy Spirit of God; are like a spigot of water ready to pour out the loving words of the Gospel!

The Spirit of God will come to all those who ask for Him to come into their lives to inform them and to counsel them on the written word of God that he put into our hearts. The one thing we must remember is we must believe whole heartedly that Jesus is the Son of God.

5. Speaking Gods word that is found in the Bible is not to be taken lightly? The word of God is given to us as His love story for all mankind for all time. In Isaiah 54:13, "and all thy children shall be taught of the Lord; and great shall be the peace of thy children."

You are being invited, to read His word so that you may respond in a way to share His word with others!

I remember a time in my science classes in high school; when the teacher went out of his way to explain what we were looking at in the sky? He tried to explain how we developed from some amoeba of certain stages? I would close my eyes and try to picture what it looked like before the creation. Can you imagine nothing coming from nothing? Then I remembered that in science we need five things to happen, 1st would be a (Time) period, 2nd some type of (Force) was needed, 3rd an (action) had to take place, 4th it had to use up some sort of(space, 5th then finally it would be formed of some (matter)?

Well, being a recent Alter Boy of five years before going into high school I thought of the word of God, that being of course the Holy Bible. I remembered the Book of Genesis. It was in the first ten words of the Word of God, where I found the answer.

1st (time) in the beginning, 2nd (force) God, 3rd (action) created 4th (space) the heavens, 5th (matter) and the earth. I love using the word of God to solve or explain a question that may come up; for instance in Hebrews 11:3 "through faith we understand that the worlds were framed by the word of God (thru the Holy Spirit) so that things which are seen were not made of things which do appear. The creation is Gods idea thru the work of His faithful servant the Holy Spirit not a borrowed or thought from someone else or from somewhere else.

6. When I chose the story of the Seven Lamps, I was looking to bring the Holy Spirit into the light? The Virgins had the right idea, they were prepared! We can't see the Holy Spirit but we can be prepared for a time when He will make Himself visible in our hearts! In John 14:16-17 we find this statement? "And I will pray the Father, and He shall give you another comforter, that He may abide with you forever." "Even as the Spirit of truth, whom the world cannot receive, because it sees Him not, neither knows Him; but you know Him; for He dwells in you, and He shall be in you."

MY HOLY SPIRIT

The Holy Spirit is an empowerment for us to be on the path of truth in order for us to follow the light of life's pathway to the kingdom of God! When the Spirit comes upon you, you will receive power and be witnesses unto the whole world if need be! The Holy Spirit will make the connection we need to see by, when the things of life appear to be in darkness.

The Spirit reminds us that the teaching of Jesus the Christ who is the light of the world; lets us see beyond the darkness of all matters, Jesus died for us on the cross and His blood was shed for our sins. Our destiny is earned by our Faith in all that has been given to us thru the Holy Spirit!

Do you remember this, in Proverbs 6-23 tells us, "for this command is a lamp, this teaching is a light, and correction and instruction are the way to life?" If we don't visualize listening to the Spirit of God we will not be able to see Him?

7. The event of Pentecost is the most exciting to me of all the visualizations. In this visualization I see red, fire, and the wings of a pure white dove all at the same time coming upon the Twelve Apostles! Have you wondered how you were chosen to be an exclusive disciple of Christ? In John 15:16, "You did not chose me, but I chose you and appointed you, so that you might go and bear fruit-fruit that will last. Whatever you ask in my name the Father will give you." The Holy Spirit is the greatest servant of God, He is the agent of God He is to fulfill the Master commands, so be aware that all that Jesus said is possible thru Gods Spirit! We tend to look for a church and a Pastor to our liking! I tell you this because the Holy Spirit is the one that leads us to this finding, just as Jesus chose us He the Spirit will fill us with what He has filled the Disciples with on that Pentecost night! We will bear the fruit that Jesus talks about because He did choose us! There is a sure way to bring out this bearing of fruit; that is a very strong prayer life. With this in mind we can't go far from the path that we are being lead to follow. The Spirit makes us aware that the fruit that Jesus wants us to bear is what was written on our hearts, and the Father will

hear our prayers prayed in Jesus name, and they will be answered! Hebrews 11:1, "Now Faith is confidence in what we Hope for and the Assurance of those things we cannot see."

We must stay frosty as my Pastor would say; follow your hearts desires and remember that, "God hold open wide His arms to fulfill all our hearts desires." Psalm 145:16.

When we speak of the Holy Trinity we see that the Father, and the Son and the Holy Spirit are all God. So when we look at the next verse found in Hebrews 11:3, I see the Holy Spirit fulfilling this statement also? "The Son is the radiance of God's Glory and the exact representation of His being." The Spirit does fulfill the revelations of God and the Son in all His actions that lead us into the light of this world. Jesus however has received the greater reward by being the inherited one of the Father, and the Spirit the one who will continue to be the Greatest Servant of God and Jesus.

ARMOR OF PROTECTION

THE FIFTH OF SEVEN STEPS

Chapter 5

———❦———

THE ARMOR OF PROTECTION

WE HOPE TO see the Holy Spirit in a way that He is to be the protector of all the knowledge given to us. We are SOLDIERS in His Army?

The only defensive weapon we will be allowed to carry is the Sword of the Holy Spirit! He carries the Armor of Protection that comes from God. He is our Commander in Chief and He will stand beside us in any invasion or assault by the evil one! The Holy Spirit uses the symbols of a soldier to enhance the Seven Images of a Spiritual Warfare Campaign.

In Ephesians 6:18, "And pray in the Spirit at all times with all kinds of prayers, asking for everything you need." In order to do this correctly, you must always be ready and never give up. You must always pray for one another!

Let us look at what a SOLDIER spells out:

S = sword of the spirit the Word of God for.
O = our wearing of the belt of truth.
L = legs of ever ready with fitted feet.
D = deliver of the Gospel of Peace.

I = Interpreter of the heart of faith as His shield.

E = ever ready helmet of salvation.

R = righteousness of the breast plate.

The Seven Ways of the Spirit as the Protector

a.   (S) We will need to get a description of the usefulness of the Holy Spirit as He pertains to our Spiritual Life by protecting us through this spiritual warfare campaign. He will appear to us in the Positive Power of Prayer; the SWORD as the WORD of God that will be needed each and every day of this war that we will be fighting. We must be ready use the full Armor of God in this battle against the evil in this world. We also must be ready at all times. In this war that we will fight as Christian Soldiers will be one we cannot afford to lose!

b.   (O) The Sword as the usefulness of the Holy Spirit and testifying to OUR use of the BELT of TRUTH, which is in our hearts where everything has been written by God, for us to know. Great will be the testimony you give or hear about from many others. The Apostles have given us the original facts of truth in the life of Christ and this was done through the Holy Spirit being in them.

c.   (L) Legs with fitted feet will enable us to speak to all those who chose to follow Him Jesus each and every day of their lives. We will share in everyone's troubles like good soldiers working alongside of the Holy Spirit of our God. We will need to please our commander in chief. Our LEGS with FITTED- FEET will always be ready to carry us on our mission of readiness.

d.   (D) He is the DELIVER of the GOSPEL of PEACE, with His protection as our comforter will be well noted as we deal with all the aspects of troubled lives. There will be people who will need our help to get-by day in and day out. Our prayers will be for all peoples of all nationalities, regardless of their background! They will be blessed as well as you for caring for them.

e.   (I) Counselor is like a lawyer, He can INVENT for us a SHIELD to give to us, (If we ask Him) those things that are within the Laws of God. He makes known to us the teaching of Jesus Christ and the commandments He left us with. He will counsel us on the things of the heart? He gives us an overall view of the Commandments of God. Let us try to make sure that each command will fit into our daily lives. The best way to remember them is what Christ Jesus said, when asked what was the greatest Commandment? He replied; "To love the Father with all your Heart, soul, strength and being, and the second one is, to love one another as He loved us".

f.   (E) Redeemer is fitting here because, He is EVER- ready, and to help us put on the HELMET of SALVATION, Jesus who died on the cross for us. And His promise to send the Holy Spirit! The Spirit will help us reclaim those truths as God has given

To us and written on our Hearts. People of truth are put in front of us to make us see the path that God has always wanted us to be on in this life.

Remember the story of Ruth, Naomi and Boaz, when he acted as their redeemer to insure that they would have someone to look after them. We have been given that opportunity to be redeemed by the body of Christ which was given for sin, and His bloodshed to wash away our sins. The Holy Spirit will enforce our beliefs in redemption thru Christ Jesus.

g.   (R) The Holy Spirit as the RIGHTEOUS one, gives us the protection of the BREAST PLATE; He is still able and willing to relay to God those things you want God to hear which you will bring added Glory unto Jesus. The Holy Spirit will make sense of anything we want to say to God, especially in our prayers. Remember when God called upon Moses to go and free the Israelites from bondage? Moses felt he was slow of speech and not adequately smart enough to talk to the Pharaoh on any request that had to be made to free all the Israelites; God filled him with the Spirit to be able to act with knowledge and wisdom making God's Glory shine before mankind.

1

DESCRIPTION OF HIS USE-FULLNESS.

a.   (S) The Sword of the spirit is in the Word of God. Every Christian needs to be ready for war, whether we want to or not? We are at war with the evil of this world, and we are Christian SOLDIERS of GOD! The Holy Spirit is ready willing and quite able to help us in all our needs. We must be Believe in all our Hopes and be secure in our Faith. Without Faith, real Faith we will lose the war of all our beliefs and they will be taken away from us. Remember back in 1962! This is when they tried taking 22 words out of the Constitution saying it was a Prayer? Then in 1980 they took the Ten Commandments out of the class rooms and public buildings.

It is these kinds of defeats that we cannot tolerate; we need to be aware of what the Positive Power of Prayer can do. We must have great Faith and ask the Holy Spirit of God to be our Commander in Chief and lead us on a pilgrimage to fight the good fight against the evil of this world. Do you remember in 1997, they stopped letting Prayer be said at Sports events, in our schools; and during commencement ceremonies? We are unable to defend ourselves because we don't band together and protest as Christian Soldiers?

As Christians we are not allowed to take the first punch so to speak. We are not being never offensive enough when it comes to protecting our rights to be able to Worship our God as He should be worshiped.

So how would the Holy Spirit lead us into battle? Well He might get us to oppose the authority causing the problems? They are out looking for the vote and the able- minority's get their attention why can't we? Once again remember this, we have Jesus and the Holy Spirit on our side Jesus said ask anything in my name and I will grant it!

We are protected against the ruling of Satan because we were pre-destined by God to accept Jesus as the Son of God when Jesus came upon us as in (John 15-16) we were considered to be exclusive when we come forward (As Re-born) when we are baptized into Christ, we will not die in the second death, so; on ward Christian Soldier's marching as to war knowing that the Cross of Jesus is our banner to lead us on the path of a victory through the Holy Spirit forever more.

Saint Paul in Ephesians chapter Six tells us to use the full Armor of God to fight against evil and to protect ourselves! This will ensure us to take a stand against evil. We must imagine a spiritual War; one that includes the full armor of God. The only offensive weapon we will use is a spiritual Sword and that is the Positive Power of Prayer. When we pray we do it with our hearts and with faith that the Word of God is our strength in fighting a spiritual battle.

Paul said in Ephesians (6:17-b), "and the Sword of the Spirit, which is the word of God." These words should cause us to remember that words of prayer are your sword and this battle against evil will make you believe you have enough faith and trust in the word of God, you can then defeat the evil one.

2

TEACHING AND TESTIFYING-

b.   (O) Teaching and testifying by wearing OUR Belt of Truth; Paul said in Ephesians 6: 19. "Pray also for me, that whenever I speak, words may be given me so that I will fearlessly make know the mystery of the Gospel." Paul is telling us of his teaching through his testimony of Jesus; this is done through the powerful Grace of the Holy Spirit!

Paul draws attention to the unseen world and makes it know to us. There is a battle against the Christians of this world, and it is a spiritual one that we fight. Our greatest weapon is the Holy word of God. There is a world that is unseen by us and it's like in another dimension, one we know exist just like there is an angel assigned to all of us and he is right there with us and like the Holy Spirit they cannot be seen.

We are all able to teach through the Power of a Testimony. Take the Apostles; they have given to us in writing what happened in that 1st century with Christ Jesus our Lord. By Faith we believe that all things they testified about are true. Thus they are teaching us the word of God which they were led by the Holy Spirit; and by the Holy Spirit we receive in faith all things are true. The proof of all things that are unseen is through Faith. We are taught to believe in the protection of the Spirit, we ask of Him and He will teach us.

In John 7:17. "If anyone's will is to do God's will, then he will know whether the teaching is from God or whether I am speaking on my own authority." The Holy Spirit will guide us to do the will of God; each Christian that sets out to do Gods will welcomes the teachings of Jesus and believes that the Spirit will be with them to guide them always. When we seek the Spirit we have understood the rewards of our Faith! Do you remember the phrase "Follow Me"; I ended my first book called; My Saviors: First: "Seven Steps - Seven Ways."

This term ("Follow Me") is a giveaway for all who come to Jesus; we are empowered with His teachings. We must then let the Holy Spirit of God bring us face to face with our Holy Father; we too shall hear not only the voice of the Spirit but that of God also!

Let's look at (Temptation) the Holy Spirit will teach us that we should not be tempted to do as the Smiths are doing? Getting new clothes, cars or buying the best quality of food for the dinner plate! We need to be frugal in our walk in life! Temptations itself are not sins. Jesus was tempted in the desert was He not? Well if you yield to them it is a sin! The Holy Spirit teaches us (paraphrased) as in the book of 1

Corinthians 10: 13. That God will not give you any temptations that will over whelm you, at least those that are common to all persons! The Holy Spirit will protect you, guide you and teach you to resist and to endure all those things that could cause you to fall.

The teachings of the Holy Spirit are unlimited; we must always be willing to call upon Him for all aspects of our lives. All of us that went to school and for those who are in school now; we have had to establish study habits? Without these habits we find ourselves doing other things that take us away from what we need to concentrate on. Without the help of the Spirit, and our prayers, we can fail in learning what God has planned for us. We were all given talents and gifts from God and we are expected to use them to the best of our abilities. Pray, Pray and Pray for help in all matters thru the Holy Spirit of God the Father Almighty. Your life will be enriched to live as Jesus lived; that should be your goal in learning.

3

SPEAKING TO COVERTS

c. (L). We must steady our LEGS with the Fitted Feet at all times to explain our readiness. This is an area that should be a goal for all of us who follow Christ our Lord through the Holy Spirit! Speaking to new Christians, teaching them, and listening to their questions; is a rare privilege for all of us. We must be prepared to help the new converts in not only accepting Christ but how to live for Him?

Do you remember in Matthew 13:10, the Disciples asked of Jesus why do you talk to the people in parables? "He answered them this way! You have been given a gift to accept those things I do and understand them; these people are like children they need a story to explain the kingdom of Heaven that is at hand?

If you were to paraphrase the word of God for new converts I'm sure they would receive the word in a way that would help them understand much better!

When Christ was teaching about the Kingdom that is to come, He was not trying to build on the foundation that the Pharisees were teaching, but on a Kingdom to come; as in the Lord's Prayer! A Kingdom that would be in itself separate and new to those who would leave this life for another one; without the body they have now but one that would be better and very spiritual. The Holy Spirit will be the one that will take us to that plain were we would seek out the teaching of Jesus.

I would love to give you this example of simplicity in talking to new converts? First the Biblical literal version! Try this, John 1:12 say's, "Yet to all who receive Him, to those who believe in His name. He gave them the right to be called the children of God."

Now a simplified version of which I call the cowboys version, "To all of you that have decided to saddle up with the Boss in Heaven; to those who believe in who they ride for. The Boss (God) gave them the right to be called His Cowboys and cowgirls and His little Buckaroos."

Paraphrasing is an art; Jesus did it so wonderfully in His parables. This is to give new converts a view that will help them understand the Word of God on their level of thinking as new believers?

The Holy Spirit will guide us to the path where we will see signs that tell us to keep away from leaders that ask us to follow them rather that the teaching of our Christ. Do you remember the parable in Luke 6-39, when He talked about the blind leading the blind? We must be very careful of following leaders that already have been rejected by others! Following someone blindly will cause you to reject the word of God; so be careful keep your eyes on your own heart and your mind on the ways of the Holy Spirit.

I also used in a message a view of the Ten Commandments as the rules of the Boss, simplified version for teaching new rules to converts!

1. We are to have only one Boss!
2. We are to love the Boss more than anything else!
3. We are to use the Boss's name with great respect!
4. We are to keep the Boss's Day very special!
5. We are to show respect for our Ma's and Paw's always.
6. We are not to use our guns to murder.
7. Let the ring on your finger remind you of your promises!
8. Stealing from others ain't right!
9. Lying is just plain wrong!
10. We must keep our eyes focused on what we own only.

I pray that you get my drift on talking to new converts keep it Biblical by all means, but simple!

This may at times challenge your assumptions in teaching the Word of God, but believe me, keeping it simple will help them to increase their Faith that all The Holy Spirit's help is as real as you and I; standing next to each-other praying over the right words to use. As we try and make new converts see the Bible in a simplified manner, so that they may become Children of God.

We need to remember this, the command Jesus gave us in Matthew 28:18, has four parts to it; first was to go forth and preach the Word, second to those who accept the Word must confess and repent of their sins, third, they are to be Baptized as in (re-birth/born), and fourthly be filled with the Holy Spirit. For this to all happen, we need to use our Fitted Feet standing our ground in teaching to the new converts to follow Jesus each and every day of their lives. Remember this He (Jesus) is the Way, truth and the life we need help in living for, because we cannot come to the Father accept by Jesus. The Holy Spirit will lead you in all your endeavors. We should be ready to share the troubles of all the new converts' troubles, like a good soldier working alongside of the Holy Spirit of God. Also we should not forget we need to please Him who is God for He is our Commander in Chief!

4

COMFORTER

d. (D) the Holy Spirit is the DELIVER of the Gospel of Peace. To be filled with the Holy Spirit is walking by Faith. Many of us can be confused in how we need to understand the filling of the Holy Spirit! The Bible really doesn't say much about this filling of the Spirit? We get to ask for the Spirit to come into our Temple of God and be our Comforter. If we look around we see many Christians that stand-out more than others, in the way they show how comfortable they are in talking, walking and living a Jesus like life! The Holy Spirit is the actual deliver of the words of the Gospel of Peace; with His protection as our Comforter, He will be with us as we deal with all aspects of our troubled lives and those of the new Converts. These people will need our help to get by, day in and day out.

The Comforter acts as our encouragement. This was noted during the 1st Century, when Christians knew they had the Spirit with-in them. They knew their old selves and they not only felt Him, they acted as Jesus would have. In Acts 9:31 we see this, "All of the Churches in the area found a Peace, and were built up, and walking in the fear of the Lord; and in the Comfort of the Holy Spirit, it was multiplied." I can just imagine the beauty of all this, especially in the working environment, worshiping the risen Lord Jesus and in their daily lives. Being filled with the Spirit does not mean we can kick back and not worry about studying the Word, no we must stay alert so that the Devil will not get a rope on us; we would then be obliged to call up the Holy Spirit to have Jesus cut the rope!

Using the Holy Spirit to prove Jesus to anyone should be in our nature! Remember this Jesus is the focus of all God's plans. The Holy Spirit assures us that our attention will be focused on Jesus this will further glorify His name with our Father which art in Heaven!

It is the will of God that everything written on our hearts by Him; be revealed to us by His Holy Spirit. So whatever question we have of the Spirit, it is said, (Romans 8:27) "the Spirit searches our heart's to make know to us all things of God."

This is probably a good time to remind ourselves that the Holy Spirit is really a person He is a He, and not an (it). You heard this old saying, the Bible told me so? We can list quite a few maybe even more than that in this book you will find (49) forty-nine of those areas that He works and guides and comforts, and even increases our intelligence to gain wisdom over all matters!

The Holy Spirit has given us all the gifts we need to last us thru our life-time. There are nine gifts as in the Fruits of the Spirit when excised complete our comfort zone to deal with anyone at any time in our lives. You remember them as we use them; Love, Peace, Joy, Patient, Goodness, Gentleness, Kindness, Faithfulness, and Self Control!

These gifts are given to mankind to lead them in all their endeavors of life and within the Church it-self. We acting as the Saints of the Church get to use them to enhance the wellbeing of the Church; by this I mean we all come together as one body. Using the gifts to work in side of the Church; we all have gifts that standout more on one person than on others. So what is lacking one can then find comfort that someone will come forward and fill in the needed gift to accomplish the needs of the Church. This also applies to preaching, ministry, and converting, and comforting those who need the Word of God to enhance their lives, in or out side of the Church.

The growth of the Church is very important, seeking young and old alike, gives us the ability to grow. The ministry outside of the Church is a must for all of us; we need to spread the Word of God to our entire community' find that these Gifts given to us by the Holy Spirit are meant to be shared in order to increase the comfort table with in the Church as well as the community. The key to success of any ministry is using the Fruits of the Spirit; we must turn others in a new direction for them to be in their comfort zone living for Christ.

5

COUNSELOR

e. (I) The Holy Spirit INTERPRETS why a Shield is to surround us shaped in the form of a Heart; to keep all the parts of our Armor of Protection within reach and to Counsel us on how to use them as SOLDIERS of the Spirit!

The Holy Spirit is not like an apple; we can see the apple, feel it, taste it, you can even hear the crunchy bite of the apple. We can-not do these things with the Holy Spirit, but He is really there. For you to be able to experience the Spirit of God you must first form a belief and the greater the belief the greater your faith will be in His presence with you.

How can we converse with the Holy Spirit? You have a Conscience that causes you to think about things as you do them? Well this is how the Spirit acts with you! The co-mingling of the Heart and the Mind, to form a conciseness and you then begin to talk with the Holy Spirit and He will counsel you in all matters.

This can be called that which God gave to you; like the Sole or a personality, it can be said that the Spirit co-mingles with the sole to give you understanding of right from wrong. The Holy Spirit gets involved to provide the assurance you will need and the redeeming qualities to forgive and to understand. He will then be able to counsel you in all matters of your decision making. He will comfort, correct, and increase your prayer quality in your hour of need. This is all done that God may then be able to understand all that you are asking for in your hour of need.

"Let your light shine before men that they may see your good works and glorify your Father." (Matthew 5-16)

Can you describe the Holy Spirit in five words or less and would they be (He is everything God is). The Holy Spirit has been promised to us by Jesus and as our Counselor He is the Holy Spirit of God. He makes know to us the Truths of the Bible, and the teachings of the Commandments of God.

How do we receive the counsel of the Holy Spirit; in five words you must do this, (He must be asked for).

God's plan for us has been the same ever since the very first day of creation; that being, for us to worship Him. We have found that a sin was committed in the Garden of Eden and this separated us from Him. His new plan became our Salvation. This was to bring us back to worshiping Him as He intended for us to do!

God came to us in the flesh as His Son Jesus; to show us we can live a life as close to that as depicted by Christ Jesus. Jesus then died upon the Cross to save all who were Lost. The promise of the Holy Spirit would be fulfilled, ("when we ask for Him"); and receive His counsel and believe that Jesus is the Son of God! We will then receive Him in our hearts and He will give us counsel to say that we believe by faith that all things are possible thru Him.

It will be by your faith that all the things that Jesus taught will be revealed threw your heart. You will then have a new life accepting the will of the Holy Spirit, and the old life of sin and the Law through self-effort will be put aside. The work of the Holy Spirit will bring a bridge for us to build upon to accomplish our efforts to worshiping God as He intended for us. The Holy Spirit brings Honor and Glory to the Son of God, our Savior and Lord Christ Jesus.

Our ability to understand and to compare the good from evil syndrome; will come to us no matter what the situation or appearance of the problem. The Counsel of the Holy Spirit will be able to put all the facts together for you to come to the right conclusion.

6

AS THE REDEEMER.

f.   (E). To be Ever Ready to accept that our Salvation is protected with the Helmet of Salvation. Are you ready to buy back your Salvation? Christ paid a price for all to be free of Sin! All we have to do is two things; 1st declare Jesus as Lord and Savior, He is the Son of God, 2nd ask the Holy Spirit to come into your life and act as your redeemer.

Christ Jesus paid a price that you and I may never be able to repeat; but Jesus did say that the greatest gift one could do was to lay one's life down for another. In Romans 6-4 we find this, we are buried with Christ in the Baptismal water and from that; as He was raised from the dead by God the Father so that we may see the Glory of Jesus that the Father has given unto Him. It is because of this redeeming fact that we to might be raised to an eternal life in Heaven.

To be redeemed by the Holy Spirit is to be redeemed by His Armor of Protection. When I was a young teenager I didn't like going to the beach, unless I was forced to do so! You see my girlfriend (Now my Wife) made me go to the beach either at Rockaway or Coney Island Beach (both in New York). I didn't like the sun; the only protection given to me was some oily stuff with Iodine in it, to protect from the Sun's rays! Later on in life (much latter) the Doctors found I had a Vitamin "D" deficiency. I (had to take 50,000 I U's of "D", after two of these I was quite sick like an overdose? (I thought I was going to die?) There has to be a better way to be protected from outside rays! We are redeemed by the protection of the use of the Armor of Protection offered by the Holy

Spirit. Not like some sun-screening oil or suntan lotion that we rub on and it dries and fades away. All His redeeming qualities are built in to the Temple of God and He makes them readily available to use when we ask for them. The Holy Spirit reminds us that it was Jesus our redeemer, with His blood, did purchase our freedom. In Ephesians 1:7, In Him we have redemption through His blood, and the forgiveness of Sins, in accordance with God's grace. The Spirit reminds us that it was not with Silver or Gold that we were redeemed but with His precious blood.

With the Helmet of Salvation the Holy Spirit protects us as it does for the SOLDIER. In this chapter the Holy Spirit is our Protector, as in the Armor of protection found in Ephesians 6. The Helmet is protection for the consciousness of the mind that stores up all our information of knowledge and the wisdom to use this knowledge. We don't have to be real soldiers as in war types but we are ready to serve God in all matters.

Ruth sent Naomi to Boaz, because she knew he would do justice by her in accordance with the Jewish Laws. The Holy Spirit put all of them together in order that the path would be formed for the lineage of Christ Jesus.

There were many men and women in the Old Testament that were filled with the Holy Spirit; they were not soldiers or army types. The Holy Spirit led them to victories and inspired them to serve the Lord. They also did not attempt to retain their power as Judges of Israel. Look at Gideon he did not want the people to make him King and he didn't want his son to be king. He said bluntly that it is God who shall rule over you. (Judges 8:23)

He also found that it was God who was their Savior. It was the Spirit of God that was active in the men and women to bring a redeeming saving power to all of Israel and for them to Rule for Him.

We have talked about Israel's religious, Spiritual and political life and that they were entwined; all related to God. Not like today when we are

Constantly trying to keep them separate as if it could be a disease and it may be contagious. Wouldn't it be wonderful if God's rules were still our rules for life on earth?

Here is an example; The United States of America was founded on the rights for all mankind; and it has been the will of God that America be the nesting place of religious freedom! In the book of Amos we find that Amos looked at Israel's religious and social life, and we find that just as it was then some (750) years before Christ it is today the injustice, immorality and idolatry of the country are going on. Amos believed if they only would all come back to the Lord in prayer, prosperity could return to the land again. This can be said of America also, we need to use the Holy Spirit of God and come together not only in prayer but in action by turning around the threats against our religious rights.

Politics of our Government is still our number-one enemy as it was in the 1st days of our founding of America when the King of England dictated what we needed to believe in.

The Holy Spirit will help us fight the good fight to go against those who are so ready to take our religious freedoms away. Here is another thought; don't vote for anyone that is not ready to stand up and fight to keep our religious rights in tack?

7

AS THE INTERPRETER –

g. (R) Our Righteousness' is to be protected by the Breast Plate; The Holy Spirit is like a bullet-proof vest that stops anything from destroying what God has written on our hearts.

As the Interpreter He is ready to pass on to God the Father Almighty; all of those things that you would want God to hear. The Holy Spirit will make sense of anything we want to say to the Lord; especially in our prayers to Him. I have found that there are Seven Ways to Praise God.

1st - Is, always remember Him on a daily basis. Put your actions where your mouth is! Ps. 34-1, "I will extol the Lord at all times; His praises will be on my lips."

2nd - Keep Holy the day of the Lord. Remember to visit Him in His House. When you come into His sanctuary be ready to give Him Praises, Honor and Glory. Ps. 100-4, "Enter His gates with thanks given and His courts with Praise, give thanks to Him and His Holy Name.

3rd - Who has your back ever-since the begging of time? Isaiah 25-1, "O Lord you are my God I will extol thee and praise your holy name. For in perfect faithfulness you have done marvelous things that were done so long ago before the creation.

4th - God does expect you to give Him praise and to thank Him for all those things you asked for and received. Isaiah 43-21, "For God created all things (and He said) the people I formed for myself that they may proclaim my praises." Like the heavens and the earth for example!

5th - Don't you wish that there was a single phone number you could call God on in heaven that would give you all the answers. 2 Samuel 22-4, "If I called to the Lord who is worthy of all praises I will then be saved from mine enemies!

6th - I ask you this, is there a correct position to call upon the Lord to pray or to give Him praises? 1 Corinthians 23-30 "the people were to stand in the morning and the evening, to give Him praise." Then there is kneeling, bowed heads, sitting, and raised hands up to the Lord in heaven. All of these for us would be fitting!

7th - How about remembering Him to others? Did not Jesus say if you do not tell others about me I will not tell the Father about you? Job 36-24, "remember to extol His work which men have praised in song."

How would you like to activate the Interpreters (Holy Spirit) Power into your life? I call it the U.S.A. movement to receiving the Spirit of God.

U- Understanding of the truths of God.

S-submission to get rid of sin.

A-acknowledgement that walking by Faith is yielding all to God.

Understanding the Gospel as in Luke 11-13, "When you ask God for the Holy Spirit God will give Him to you because whether you are good or evil, but you give your children good things God will respect you". Luke 9-23, "Take up your cross on a daily basis," Especially if you want to live a Christ like life as Jesus did. The Holy Spirit is here to be an interpreter, advocate, to guide and to convict you in all your judgments!

Submission in order to get rid of sin, by confessing and repentance! Let us look at 1 John 1-9, "If we confess our sins! He is faithful and just and will forgive us our sins. He will purify us from un-righteousness!" If we are to view God's mercy, by offering our bodies as a living sac-rifice, as we hold the Temple of God within us and the Holy Spirit resides there; it will be Holy and pleasing unto worshiping God.

Acknowledgement First of all we need to count on our faithful believing as we are baptized in the water we are dead to sin and alive to God the Father almighty, threw the Holy Spirit. He is ready to help us in this. Romans 6-11, "In the same way count yourselves dead to sin and alive to God." By faith we are alive to the light of His Holy Word.

CHAPTER 5 SUMMARY
ARMOR OF PROTECTION

I have tried to present to you a different view of the Holy Spirit, in order to make Him as real as possible to each of you! To me He is like the man of steel, Superman, Batman, Flash Gordon ;(so to speak of) and even a Sherlock Holmes. I used Ephesians 6:10-18, as the ultimate Protector of all believers; against all forces and by all means possible.

We discovered that we are soldiers in the Army of the Lord; with the Holy Spirit as our Commander in Chief. We can actually fight against Evil with the help of the Armor of Protection of the Spirit.

I spelled out the word <u>SOLDIER</u> and matched each letter with parts of the Protective Armor.

We have found that the only defensive weapon is the **S**word of the Spirit it represents the word of God. Put **On** the Belt of Truth using our conscious mind to inspire and instruct us. Then we use a part of our body to move us forward **L**egs to move our feet to perform for us. We find that He is the **D**eliverer of the Gospel of Peace. Then we have the Holy Spirit as an **I**nterpreter giving a shield of faith covering our Heart. We have to be **Ever** ready to put on the Helmet of Salvation. We complete this is **R**ighteousness of a SOLDIER'S Breast Plate as a bullet proof- vest.

a.   How can we describe the Holy Spirits Use-Fullness? Every Christian needs to be ready for War, whether we want to or not. We must continue to believe in all our hopes and we will be secure in our Faith. Without real faith we can lose the war against the dark forces of evil. It is the aspect of defeat that we should not tolerate. We must have great faith in the Holy Spirit as our Commander in Chief. Remember this that the Words of prayer are our weapons against all things evil. The Sword of the Spirit is the Word of God the more that you believe this you will have great faith. We are to use the full Armor of God as found in Ephesians chapter 6, against evil in order to protect our Soul. We must imagine the spiritual war that is going on all around us; with the Positive Power of Prayer.

b.   One of the gracious attributes of the Holy Spirit is to teach us and to enable us to Testify to His wonders and those of Christ Jesus that can be found written on our hearts. We are to pray for ourselves thru the Holy Spirit whenever we cannot seem to find the right words to ask for prayer or to praise God. It is through His teaching to us that will correct all your words before they ever reach God. There is a Spiritual battle going on and it comes from an unseen spirit world. When we give a testimony to others we are actually teaching just as the Apostles did. All the words of the Apostles are our Faith the more we believe they are true the greater the Faith we will have! Remember this in John 7:17, "If any ones will is to do God's will he will know whether the teaching is from God or whether I am on my own authority." The teaching of the Holy Spirit is unlimited we must call out to Him and our lives will be enriched to live as Jesus lived.

c. If anyone thinks that praying without help is hard; try Speaking to a new Convert! There can be the fear of giving them the wrong information that would cause them to go astray; and for sure you will be in deep trouble. The Five Fold Mission that Jesus gave to us was to produce five types of missionary's to spread the word of God.

First to the Apostles; Second to those who can Prophesize, Third to be Evangelist as Pastors, Fifth to be Teachers, (A.P.E. P.T.). Those who teach falsely (Mark 12-38) will be punished most severely more than other sinners for miss-guiding any-one using the Word of God. We must always ask the Holy Spirit to guide us to a path that will lead us to the signs that will give us direction in our quest to spread the Holy Word of God. We must be careful of outside forces such as our government, whether it's a church body not following the Word of God, or a City, County, State or Federal Government, or even the (U.N.) United Nations; making laws not abiding by the God's Word. So we must be careful to keep your eyes, your heart and your mind on the ways of the Holy Spirit of God. I used a simplified message of how to present the Ten Commandments to those struggling to understand them I prayed over this adaptation; I felt no pressure that I will be excommunicated from God. Keeping the word Holy for those who are about to become new children of God is my goal. We should always remember that our Commander in Chief is the Holy Spirit follows Him.

d. I just love it when the Post office delivers to me a package that is un-damaged; my Comfort level goes way up. So too when the Holy Spirit acts as our Deliver of the Gospel of Peace, I can walk Comfortably by my Faith knowing that He has my back, mind and my thoughts.

We can be as strong as the 1st Century Christians who to me had no problem knowing they were being led by the Holy Spirit. They knew what kind of life they lead in their old selves; and now they are walking on water so to speak. However being led by the Spirit does not mean we can kick back and not worry. We must continue to be studying the Word of God; lest the Devil be given a chance to throw a rope around us and try to keep us for himself. Remember this we must be obliged to call upon the Holy Spirit and have Him send Jesus to cut the rope leading us astray.

I believe that we have the greatest Comfort zone in anything we do, in this life; let us look at the value found in three passages in the Word of God! 1st in Ephesians 1-11, God predestined all of us as to what He wanted us to be in this world. We are to show conformity with His purpose of our lives. 2nd in John 15-16, Jesus was to find each of us and we were to come to Him and this makes us exclusive, He found us and we accepted Him. 3rd in Romans 8-27, The Holy Spirit searched our hearts to make those things know to us that were of God! Remember this we are to share all that we have and were given by God, Jesus, and the Holy Spirit; this is done that we might increase the Comfort level within the Church of God.

e.   When I was young (really young) I tried to make a solution that would make things water proof; I told my dad about it and put his watch in the bag I coated with the solution, then stuck it in the sink full of water. It actually sat there for a second or three, and then began to sink. My dad reached for the bag before it went to the bottom. Needless to say my invention didn't work. We can come up with many ideas to protect ourselves in this walk of life? There is only one person who can fill that solution!

The Holy Spirit's spiritual Invention of a SHIELD in the form of a Heart would surround us. This Shield is Our Armor of Protection that keeps safe all of the parts we need to act as Soldiers of the Spirit. He will then be able to counsel you in your entire decision making.

There were two five word definitions that I chose one was, how do we receive the Holy Spirit? Answer is, "He must be asked for", so that we may receive the counsel we need. The second is how can I describe the Holy Spirit? "He is everything God is". The promise of the Holy Spirit was fulfilled when Jesus ascended into Heaven. It will be by our Faith that all things of God will be revealed to us and those that Jesus taught us. The Holy Spirit that dwells within our hearts and in the Temple of God will reveal to us all things.

f.   We are to be ever ready to accept the Holy Spirit, we need to put our old lives behind us and come to the Cross where Christ died for all of us. Our Salvation is protected by the Helmet of Salvation. I once learned the Salvation Poem (by Billy Graham) "Jesus you died upon the cross" and "rose again for the lost", I found this portion of the poem leads me to two declarations? 1st Declare Jesus is Lord and Savior and the Son of God. 2nd Ask the Holy Spirit to come into your life to act as your Redeemer!

With the Helmet of Salvation the Holy Spirit protects us as the helmet of a military Solder would do. The Spirit protects our conscious mind that stores up all the information God has put there. Be ready to serve God in all matters; as a real military soldier would.

The Holy Spirit can arrange a new path in life for you as it was predestined. Remember the story of Ruth, Naomi and Boaz, the Holy Spirit guided all of them to come together and Boaz would do what was expected of him in accordance with Jewish Law. With His guidance He redeemed them and from that marriage the lineage of Christ Jesus began.

We then found many men and women, that were led by the Spirit in battle and neither of them were Soldiers or Army types. They weren't trained for war but they won the battles thru the help of the Holy Spirit.

The Holy Spirit makes us ever ready to fight for our freedom; instilling in us the fact that we were saved through Christ Jesus shedding of blood. He protects us using all that is available in the Armor of Protection.

To appreciate our redemption remembers that we were once slaves to sin and now we are free and new servants of our Lord Jesus; and under the protection of the Holy Spirit.

g. As the Interpreter the Holy Spirit passes on those prayers of a Righteous person. James 5:16, tells us "the prayer of a righteous person is powerful and effective". He is ready to pass on to God all those things that you want God to hear. Remember the Seven Way to Praise God? 1st was remember God on a daily basis, 2nd to keep holy the Day of the Lord, 3rd He is who has your back (your six) ever since the beginning of time. 4th God is waiting every day for your praises and thank you. 5th We look for a phone number to get answers from God; all we have to do is speak thru the Holy Spirit He has your number, 6th A praying position does not matter, all of the positions are to be fitting, 7th Spread the word to all who will listen that Jesus Christ is lord!

Then we activated the Power of the U.S.A,

U-To understand all about the Truths of God, believe, you will receive.
S-To Submit when you repent of your sins. Take up your cross daily.
A- Acknowledge all of your blessing with great Faith.

In 2 Timothy (3&4) we can get an impression of what a good soldier needs to be like and do. For instance I know two people who put on the full Armor of God; thru the Holy Spirit my Pastor Ralph and his wife Monica the Minister of music. They are always looking after the congregation in the teaching of God's word! They show Patience's, love, endurance, Faith, protection and understanding of the needs of others. They express how to use the full Armor of the Holy Spirit of God. They have both taken to heart to preach the Word of God to all who have been chosen by His predestination of who will receive Christ our Lord and Savior. Everyone needs a role model to follow and I have chosen them as my tutors. We need more soldiers for God's Army and more examples to lead us in battle. I pray that you will find leaders of the word of God as I have.

GIVING LIFE

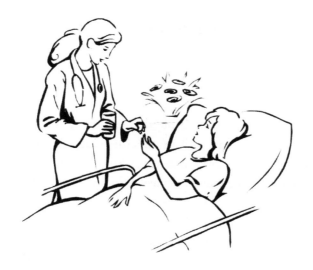

THE SIXTH OF SEVEN STEPS

Chapter 6

———— ∿ ————

As He is able to give us Life

THERE ARE MANY Verses in the Bible that can explain who and how the Holy Spirit can give us life! I chose this one (Luke 2:25-27) And there was a man in Jerusalem whose name was Simeon; and he was righteous and devout, looking for the consolation of Israel; and the Holy Spirit was upon him. And it had been revealed to him by the Holy Spirit he would not see death before he had seen the Lords Christ. And he came to the Temple by the way of the Spirit; and when the parents brought in the child Jesus, to carry out for Him the custom of the Law as required of males! Simeon took the child in his arms and blessed Him and the Lord for revealing to him the Messiah as promised.

Mankind was first formed from the dirt, and the Spirit of God breath in him to give life. Jesus on the other hand came thru God's Spiritual encounter with the Virgin and she bore life; the life of God's only begotten Son. The Holy Spirit of God can and does give us the life that we will need to encounter all things of this world.

a. To lead a Spirit Filled Life is not easily done? But God makes this promises to us; He wants us to fellowship with us and we intern are to fellowship with others about His giving of life. In Luke 4-1 Jesus came up out of the water filled with the Holy Spirit and the Spirit led Him around the wilderness and He was able to defeat the Devil.

b. With the Spirit of Grace we can find a peace free from sin! In Acts 2-38; Peter said to them "Repent", and each of you are to be baptized in the name of Jesus the Christ for the forgiveness of your sins; and you will receive the gift of the Holy Spirit. We will be free from slavery of the power of Satan as long as we are ready to repent of our sins.

c. The power of the Spirit of Adoption comes to us through Abraham; (we) (you and I) are to receive everything God promised to Abraham!
Genesis 22:15-16; Tells us that because of the willing sacrifice that Abraham was willing to commit to; the offering of his only son as a living sacrifice to God the Father Almighty ; God was very impressed and held back Abrahams hand from striking the child. At this moment God knew that Abrahams Faith was truly with God.

d. The Spirit of His Holiness and thru the power of God the Holy Spirit of God gives us a chance at new life! In Revelations 22:12-13; we find that holiness of God is to be fulfilled through Gods Spirit. "Look I am coming soon and my reward is with me"; we will be reward in-accordance to what we have done. Plus there is Genesis 1-1 "In the beginning God created the Heavens and the Earth"; we know now that the Holy Spirit is the greatest servant of God He did what God commanded Him to do; Revelations 21-1 Saint John said this; "I saw a new Heaven and a new Earth descending". (Note that they both have 10 words).

e. How He gives us Supplication. As we go to God the Father in Prayer or to His Son Christ Jesus, or the Holy Spirit; we can pray for many reasons; we can come to worship Him, or confess our sins, to ask for forgiveness, to thank Him for all His Blessing He gave us, or to ask for things for ourselves and even pray for the needs of others! There are many places in the Bible given as examples. When we read the Psalm's of David we can see how his prayers are filled with supplication; and with mercy and for strength and forgiveness.

f.   How the Spirit stands for Truth. We have seen in the Gospel that the word of God comes to us through the Holy Spirit; and whatever we need to say to God or even others we pray for the advice of the Holy and HE will guide us in our conversations whether in spiritual conversation or talking verbally to others! (2 Peter 1-21) "For no prophecy ever made by acts of a human will, but men moved by the Holy Spirit spoke from God!

g.   He is able to show us God's Glory. In the Old Testament the Holy Spirit came upon humans only by God's doing. He filled those that He wanted to have the Spirit. (Micah 3-8) "I am filled with (Glory) Power-with the Spirit of the Lord-and with Justice and Courage."

1

LIVING SPIRITUALLY

a. The Holy Spirit gives us life just as God wants us to have life with a spiritual meaning. He will do this as He did when God asked Him to remove the water from the formless and void earth in the beginning of creation. Our life is all about worshiping God each and every day of our lives. In Job 27-3 he said "For as long as life is in me, and the breath of God is in my nostrils." You see that is life as God gives us breath through the Holy Spirit He is the Breath of Life. As long as there is life in me the Holy Spirit as the breath of life is in me. Job 32-8, "But it is a spirit in man, and the breath of the Almighty that gives them understanding." As in the creation the Holy Spirit's breath gives us understanding of the wisdom that human's need to reveal to others the emotional aspects of a God giving life.

I was reading my Economics magazine one day and came across an article so misplaced I had to read it. This was written by Tom Hone; "He said that Sampson is not a copycat of the modern day suicide bomber syndrome." Instead we see that he was a victim of a woman named Delilah who was a lying callous lover, who managed to rob him of his strength and his sight. He in turned flipped the table and paid them in kind for their treachery. Sampson had been working thru the Holy Spirit that filled his soul and gave him his strength. The Holy Spirit left his consciousness for a while but not completely. Sampson begged the Lord to save him and return his strength and he would bring down the Philistine's the ones who sought to take life away from him and the Israelites. The Spiritual life of Sampson was restored and he did bring the temple crashing down and killed many Philistine's. Remember Romans 8-31; If God is for us who can be against us. God did not spare His Son from the cross; why would He not give to us anything we ask for. No one should dare to bring charges against us His chosen people. You have been declared not guilty of sin. In Acts 3, Peter was seen restoring a lame beggar's body back to life. People came running from all over to see this miracle. Peter was doing the same thing Jesus would have done and it is all by the Power of the Holy Spirit; that we do these things of God. Peter reminded them that it was by their actions that Jesus was put to death and it was the Power of God that raised Him from the dead and gave Him new Life. It is by Faith in the name of Jesus that we have healed his lameness and restored to him a better life.

Jesus in His earthly life was known to be related to the throne of David. He was born of a Virgin and was appointed to be the Son of God. When Jesus rose from the dead He was given the Power to be the Messiah our Lord. This indicates the Divineness of Jesus and the beginning of the apostolic life. Are you looking for a new life; let us look at Romans 1:5-6

"Through Him we received grace and Apostleship, to call all the Gentiles to the obedience that comes from Faith for His name's sake. And you are also among those Gentiles who are called to belong to Jesus." God has predestined each of us to be found by Jesus. We are therefore considered exclusive in accordance with John 15-16; "You did not chose me, I chose you, and appointed you, so that you may go and bear fruit."

In the book of Acts we find the Holy Spirit filling the Apostle's on a daily basis to continue in evangelizing to all they come across; even though the persecutions and troubles were all around them. Paul was filled with Joy in preaching the resurrected Christ. All of Paul's converts were also filled with the same Joy that came from the Holy Spirit. This evangelizing was done to the Glory of Jesus.

A unique thing about the book of Acts is that it is filled with more action then the rest of the Testament's; these writing and witnessing of the Spirit proves He was just as real and personal as our Lord Jesus was presented. In 1 Thessalonians 5-19, we find this verse, "Quench not the Spirit"; this to me is a warning not to take a lackadaisical attitude of worshiping God, not using the Gifts of the Spirit to enhance the Church as it goes forward. If you are filled with the Spirit is careful that you do not quench the fire it started with in you to share your gifts with every-one. A wrong attitude will also quench the Spirit we must try to prove what we say and do.

2

SPIRIT OF GRACE

b. Because of the Grace of God we have received a full pardon! Every day of our lives we face judgment because we break God's Laws. We fall short of what His Holiness demands of us. But there is a wonderful comfort that comes to us, it is God speaking through His Holy Spirit that upholds His Word and His Grace given to us through Christ Jesus; it is because ,His dying on the cross we have received a full pardon of our sins.

Ephesians 2:5-7, tells us, except for the Grace of God there go I. God has raised us up with Jesus and has given us a room in His heavenly home. It is because of the Holy Spirit that we can be reminded of God's richness and we have been given to His fullness of Grace. This is all possible because of His love for Christ and by His Grace we have been saved.

Grace should be considered as great joy, delight, sweetness, mercy, all of these could be considered the kindness of the Grace of God. The Holy Spirit will secure these feeling with-in us that we may enjoy all that Jesus promised each of us.

When Jesus died on the cross, God raised Him from the Dead; He then made a place for Him at His right hand in Heaven. In Acts 5:31-32, "God exalted Him to His own right hand, and as Prince and Savior, He might bring Israel to repentance and forgive them of their sins. (32) We are witness of these things and so is the Holy Spirit, whom God has given to those who have asked for Him". All testimonies we give can be confirmed by the Holy Spirit; it is His job to convict the world through the word of God, He is given to those who respond to our God in faith and by obeying His holy words, and believing that Jesus is the Son of God. It is by God's grace that we have been given a new chance in life.

We are to be held accountable for all our actions here on earth; and for those appointed over us will be held to an even higher standard. This is because they can inflict punishment on us for not doing what we are told.

Remember this except for His Grace there go I.

Have you ever caught yourself saying, "Except for the Grace of God there go I." We are all looking for justice no matter what the case may be or the circumstances are? You and I are to be held accountable for all our actions in our lives. There is an even greater standard set for those who teach, those who are in positions of responsibility; especially if they lead others into doing wrong. When people of leadership take advantage of those who are not able to comprehend all matters at hand and break them down to do immoral, illegal, or unjust things in their lives; they will pay dearly for their actions! We must be careful of what is preached at the Pulpit; as to the morals of God's Laws verses the ways of the world?

Do you remember the saying (W.W.J.D) What Would Jesus Do? If only! One would just ask that of them, before they take action that it just might matter; I know we have (Free Will) but shouldn't God's ways be our ways? (Yes! But!) The Holy Spirit invites us to be a part of God's plans and the writings of Jesus each and every day of our lives.

It would appear that we have many situations going on today that weren't as visible in the past; like self-serving vigilantes, those who are trying to create new laws, verses those who are to uphold the law, and those who have to obey the law's; it's like they are trying to force their own idea of a god for the times? They hide behind a god that does not exist; they hide behind a code of silence. There are those that hide behind the power of office; interpreting the Bible we all know to be the Word of God, they change it to satisfy those who don't believe the word is for them and are telling us it's ok to sin that God didn't mean for it to say what it does say!

Being a Christian does not protect us from the evil ways or the persecutions of this world. For those who believe that Jesus is the Son of God or those believe He is the greatest Prophet ever, Jesus gives us this; Luke 12:48; "from everyone who has been given much, much will be demanded; and for the one who has been entrusted with much, much more will be asked." 1 Timothy 3:1 "from everyone who aspires to be an overseer and desires to seek a noble task let them be above reproach". This is for our Church leaders, President, Supreme Justices, Lawyers, self-serving individuals, Police Officers and those in our own families and work place.

Let us remember, "except for the Grace of God go I.

In Ephesians 2; we were made alive through the Grace of God. Gods purpose has come full circle; from Adam to Jesus. All that God wanted to accomplish through the Human race was made visible when the Christ died for us on the cross! We would not be able to say by the Grace of God I have been saved; not without our Lord Christ Jesus sacrifice for all of our sins, the whole world's sins. We have Jesus to thank for our eternal future to live in Gods Heaven here on earth! It is by God's Grace and kindness that we have been saved, giving us yet another chance to present ourselves wholly and true through Christ Jesus blood on the cross.

The wrath of God passes us by, our sins are forgiven, it is by His Grace we have been freed. Each of us must have Faith that we were raised up with Christ and that it is by God's Grace not of our own; but through the gift of God, and not by anything we may have done in the form of works, or gifts or donations to anyone cause! When we do good works we do it because of the teaching of our Lord Jesus; those things that God has predestined each of us to do in our life here on earth. Remember this "we pass this way only once in life and we need to get it right the first time".

Let us be motivated in the use of our many Gifts of God, it is said all good things come from God. I love these two, for God so loved the World He gave His only Son to us; In turn we gained the right to be with God for all eternity, eternal life. Romans 12: 6-16, His Grace given to us to meet the needs of the Church; like Prophecy, Teaching, Serving, Giving, Mercy, love, Sharing and Blessing to show how we can use the Holy Spirit in our daily lives. Grace given is Grace accepted and used for our daily lives.

3

AN ADOPTION PASS –

c. In Hebrews 6:13-15, we can see that our adoption into the Promise of God's covenant that we get to receive God's Blessing right along with Abraham. I give thanks to Abraham and to Jesus in insuring us we have been given the opportunity in sharing the promises and the blessing of the Covenant promised to all the descendants of Abraham. There are two unchangeable blessing found in Genesis 22:15-17, first is the Covenant of God and the second is the Oath Sworn to by God and His very Being! There no one else higher than God the Father Almighty so He swears by and off Himself!

The Holy Spirit of God confirms and convicts us of every word of God's Covenant. He dwells in us and assures us that God's blessing is very much ours through our Faith in Him. The Spirit of God speaks to our spirit given to us as soon as we became life in our mother's womb!

Romans 8:14-17, "For as many as are led by the Spirit of God, these are the Sons of God. For you did not receive the spirit of bondage again to fear, but you received the Spirit of Adoption by whom we cry out, "Abba,*Father,' the Spirit Himself bears witness with our spirit that we are children of God, and if children, then we are heirs-heirs of God and joint heirs with Christ, if indeed we suffer with Him, that we may also be glorified together."

As God is our creator He is then truly our Father, since all of creation was done by the Faithful Servant of God the Holy Spirit; everything has been created in and with Love. All of these things we have accepted in the Adoption through Abraham and of Jesus.

We find in Matthew 5:45, that God shows His love to all people good and evil alike. When it rains it rains on all people in all lands. But in John 8:44 we see that those who don't believe that Jesus was sent by God they are the children of Satan who is the father of all lies. Jesus said that they belong to another father he is the devil. You must have Faith to be mine.

It is God's will that we obtain an inheritance, He has predestined all who receive Jesus and who work to a purpose of obeying His will through His Holy Spirit. When you first heard the Gospel of Jesus the Christ you then have accepted the word of Truth and the way to your salvation. Then you who have believed are also sealed with the Holy Spirit of God. This is all a part of the Promise that guarantee's our inheritance until the time of our redemption. We should be ever thankful of all the Jews that did not understand why Jesus came and they did not believe He was the Messiah.

I don't believe that any of us would be able to come to the saving Grace that Jesus bought for us with His dying on the cross! We were predestined to accept the Messiah; I see it this way, and this is done thru the Holy Spirit of God, God had fore-knowledge of all of us; this meaning that before time ever began He knew every spirit that would ever be born, and when Jesus came with the Gospel of God we were predestined to accept Jesus the Messiah when He called for us to follow Him. We therefore were considered to be Exclusive, (John 15-16). Jesus enabled us to bear good fruit and then when we pray the Father will hear our prayers because we have asked it in the Name Jesus. Remember the Holy Spirit teachers us all things of God and He convicts us to be able to do the right thing.

We have been given an Adoption Pass that gives us the right to by-pass the Wrath of God? Think of it this way; there is a very large forest fire approaching your camp ground in the middle of a forest! There is no way out of the fire danger, all roads are blocked? How can you protect your- self from the fires of hell? Surely you are about to burn up and all around you, material things and other lives. We call out for help ask others to aid us, what is the solution to be saved? One way is to set a fire to all that is around you clean up the area burn what is loose now; if we repent of our sins we then make a way for the fire of hell to stop before it reaches you! Look at it this way, Jesus is the only righteous Son of God He took the on flames of Hell (voluntarily) for your sins and mine, for the whole world for that matter. When we come to the cross we will be protected and not get burned. The Holy Spirit will once again convict us of these things. Jesus ensures us of the Grace of God through the Adoption By-pass.

4

HOLINESS

d. "and through the Spirit of Holiness was appointed the Son of God in power by His resurrection from the dead; Jesus Christ Lord. Romans 1:4 this is without a doubt a proclamation that Jesus is the Son of God. It is the divine nature of things that we receive our apostolic proclamation.

Without a doubt we have all been called to be disciples of Jesus. Just think if Jesus had not come when He did we wouldn't have the New Testament and no inkling of what God wanted of us, we would be just like the Israelites waiting for the Messiah! The Holy Spirit gives us life in the words of the Gospel; they show us the past, present and the future. We are now servants unto Jesus in order to spread the word to all peoples and all nations. We have been commissioned by Christ to give the life giving water for all who wish to be saved.

I'm glad that I was born when I was; my life didn't start out with God, or Jesus or even the Holy Spirit in mind. My conviction through His Holy Word and the confessing of my sins and my baptism and the receiving of the Holy Spirit was without a doubt the most fantastic day of my life. The Holy Spirit breath into me a new life giving me a chance not to save only my soul but any who would hear the word of the Gospel. I have had road blocks put in front of me, but for the Grace of God, I survived.

I am told that all Christians are Holy; we have been set apart by Gods predestination. We are beings that are an experiment of God, and being made holier each day of our lives! This is done with the asking of the Holy Spirit to be with us, comfort us, teach us and guide us in all matters. I think that the greeting of one another in the (OT) was fabulous it went like this, "with Grace and Peace I greet you." Plus Paul and the other Apostles said this, "I come as a servant of Christ Jesus". We must set the correct back-ground as to who's calling we belong to. We go calling in the name of the Father and of the Son and the Holy Spirit.

Where is the most Holy place that you would like to be at today or tomorrow or the Day of the Lord? Revelations 22:1-2, gives us a picture of what life giving Holiness is all about. This is given to you from the Holy Spirit as He shows us in our minds how these words can form a picture; something like back in Chapter 4 use of the Visual Symbols as presented in your mind through the Holy Spirit.

Will Eden be restored? "Then the angel showed me the river of the water of life, as clear as crystal, flowing from the throne of God and of the Lamb. It flowed down the middle of the great street of the city. On each side of the street stood the tree of life, bearing twelve crops of fruit, yielding its fruit each month. And the leaves of the tree are for healing of the nations." It would appear that God has restored the Holiness of Eden as it was intended for all of mankind; and those who would accept Christ Jesus as His Son. What could be more Holier and pictures' than this vision that the Holy Spirit gives us Holiness! I can see all of the previous Chapters depicted in this verse can you? i.e. The Servant of God, the Elements, His Power or His Symbols, His Teaching instead of Armor of Protection, the current chapter and then our Quest in the use of the Holy Spirit.

Deuteronomy 26:18-19, "The Lord today has declared you to be His people, a treasured possession, as He promised you, and that you should keep all His commandments; and that He will set you high above all nations which He has made, for the praise, frame, and honor; and that you shall be a consecrated people to the Lord your God as He has spoken."

We are His treasured possessions made holy thru the belief in Christ and with the knowledge of the Holy Spirit.

With the scenes we imagine, we can see that the promises of God made to Israel on Mont. Sinai. Abraham, and being grafted in to the tree of life what more proof do we need that we are His holy people and that it was because we asked for the Holy Spirit to come into our lives and He will ask God to reveal to us those deep things of God one day.

We need to look at this verse in 1 Peter 1: 15-16," But like the Holy one that called you, be holy yourselves also in all your behavior; because it is written, You Shall Be Holy Because I Am Holy." We are exclusive all who reside on earth and believe our new home will be in Heaven.

5

PRAYER OF SUPPLICATION –

e.   In the Supplication of Prayer we will see the most important role the Holy Spirit of God will play in our lives; at least by my standard of understanding. You see Jesus said He would ask the Father to send to us His Holy Spirit that we may communicate with Him (God the Father). The processes of how we can talk to God is fulfilled by our ability to ask for the Spirits help in all matters; especially in our prayer request for those times in our lives that we may need help. If we were to go to the Book of Psalms we will find that King David made many request, petitions, and supplications for others, for certain situations, for himself, and the Nation of Israel.

This brings us to where or who do we go to for problem solving? We go to God for praising Him and to worship Him, to confess our sins, to ask for His forgiveness, to thank Him for His Blessing , all our unsolvable situations; not only for us but on behalf of others and our country.

So the crucial aspect in the act of prayer is the use of the supplication (request) and our Faith, we must have faith that all matters will be resolved sooner or later! The Holy Spirit has been appointed to be our intercessor in all these matters.

I would like to look back to Chapter 5; there we found the use of the Holy Spirit in the Armor of protection. We found as He is our Commander in Chief we are His Soldiers, and He gave us tools to use to protect us; but we can and should use the Power of the Prayer of Supplication whenever we need the Holy Spirit to act on our behalf. We must be alert enough to pray to the Spirit of God in making and using supplication for all who you pray for. These prayers are used to fight off any and all spiritual wars coming against us or those we pray for. When we pray for a peace to calm our anxieties remember this; "God's Peace which passes all understanding, will guard our hearts and minds, in His Son Christ Jesus." (Philippians 4:7) Our faith in Jesus leads us to stronger faithful; prayers. We are looking for more than a mindful attitude, something like an inner peace with our God. If we are trying to apologize to God for our sins, it should take on a form of repentance, not to do this sin again; to act with sincerity just as we believe that the Armor of God protects us so does the righteousness' of those who pray!

Philippians 4:6, "do not be anxious about anything but in every situation, by supplication of prayer with thanksgiving, let your request be known to God." We cannot be self-centered or anxious as it is, because it is not faith proving of Jesus's word. If we are to act as Disciples we must show concern but have faith that our prayers will be answered in every situation we pray about. We cannot show anxiety this helps defeat those things we are asking for in our thanksgiving prayers. We must not be worrying, about answer or if anything will come of our prayers. This is where our Faith in Christ Jesus comes into play, either you believe or you doubt. I personally would rather believe that all my prayers will be answered; I wish it was in my time but we must remember that it will be done in God's time!

Ask yourself this question; what do you assume God wants when you pray or come to worship Him? The Israelites used burnt offering, they were consumed completely by the fire on the altar. Who eats ashes? Not me, nor does God, but that's what He expected back then. How about offering your first born child? Abraham was ready to commit to God His first born son of Sarah their Isaac. When Moses was assigned to have God's people get out of Egypt God had the Angel of death come across the land and cause the death of everyone's first born son, including animals. God took King David's first born son for David's sin. God showed us that He was willing to sacrifice His first born Christ Jesus, (He Did) this was for you and I that our sins would be forgiven and forgotten! So how can we please God when we come to pray to Him and to worship Him? God has made know to all that He wants nothing; but from us; just to live in peace and harmony with each other and to Praise His holy name. You want to walk with God change your lifestyle and praise Him each and every time you ask of Him in prayer and supplication those things that will make your life, or someone else's life better. Do you want to walk the walk with Jesus then walk humbly? We can pray and praise Him at the same time! In my class I taught on the Seven Ways to Praise God! I list them here for you to see.

1. We must always remember Him daily. Put your actions where your mouth is. Psalm 34-1, "I will extol the lord at all times. His praises will be on my lips," (always).

2. Keep Holy the Sabbath, visit Him in His house, and when you come through the doors of His sanctuary be ready to give to Him all is due him, like praises, Honor, and Glory. Psalm 100-4, "Enter His Gates with thanksgiving and His courts with Praises, and give thanks to Him and praise His Holy name."

3. Who has your back ever since the beginning of time? Isaiah 25-1-b, for in perfect faithfulness you have done marvelous things, things that were done so long ago. (Before Creation Even).

4. Let us give to God praises and blessing of thanks given for all those things that were asked for and received; Isaiah 43-21, God created all things, " He said, "mankind was created for Him-self, that they may proclaim my praise." like those things He created in the heavens and on the earth.

5. Would you like answers to things by calling upon God? If there was one phone number to call God would you use it? 2 Samuel 22-4; "I called to the Lord who is worthy of Praise I will then be saved from mine enemies."

6. Is there a correct position to praise or pray to the Lord? 1 Corinthians 23-30; the people were expected, to stand in the morning and in the evening to give Him praises and to pray." (Today we can bow our heads, kneel, or use the sitting position).

7. How we remember Him to others. Job 36-4, "remember to extol His works which men have praised in song." Then there was what Jesus reminds us to do with all we have learned from the word of God?

   Jesus said in Luke 12-8, "Who-ever confesses me before mankind, him shall I confess before the angels of God."

In our prayers of supplication we can find a peace that comes only through the Holy Spirit of God. When we attend a church service we come to God as we speak to one another, in the opening addressing of where we are, in the opening prayer, in spiritual songs and hymns and in Psalms. All of these can create a spiritual feeling of wanting to sing our hearts out.

I love this Psalm 103:1-5; "Bless the Lord oh my soul, and all that is within me Bless His holy name. Bless the Lord, oh my soul and for-get none of His benefits; Who pardons all your iniquities, Who heals all your disease; Who redeems your life from the pit, Who crowns you with loving-kindness and compassion; Who satisfies your years with good thing. So that your (life) is like an eagle."

Let us all thank God that we can sustain our lives through the holy Power of prayer. I thank God for my Savior Jesus who asked God the Father for His Holy Spirit will be sent to all who ask for Him.

6

TRUTH REWARDED

f.   Let us seek the goodness (Truth) and not evil. Then the Lord God Almighty will be with you; just as you proclaim He is. (Amos 5-14). Too many times we find people trying to come up with a get rich skim; they use deceit to cheat others out of their life saving. These kinds of people ignore all the decent warning of not to hurt others. They will live with the horror and consequences of all their actions. God will not overlook misguided deeds of hurting those who are vulnerable like the poor, elderly, or the innocent.

The Spirit of Truth is the Holy Spirit; He is just as real to me as Jesus and of Gods place in me and this world. He is in essence the action spirit; He is ready to get things done for us as we seek the blessing of God and the understanding of the testament of Jesus. All three persons of the Holy Trinity are of the Spirit of Truth! First there is God's word!

(2 Timothy 3:16-17)All scripture is inspired by God; we use His words to teach others, to train them to be disciples of righteousness, and for correcting our path in life. This is done that mankind maybe adequately prepared for good works. Second there is the works of Jesus!

(John 14-6) "I am the way and the truth, and the life: no one comes to the Father (God) but through me. (Jesus). Third the Holy Spirit, that is within us.

(John 16-13). "But when He the Spirit of Truth comes He will guide you into all the truth: for He will not speak on His own initiative, but will disclose to you what is to come".

All who call upon the Holy Spirit are ready to lead a new life in the Spirit; we are ready to put our old life behind us and the Old ways of the Law aside and put all our sins in the past. When I look back in time and see just how the Apostles and their Disciple lived their lives in the Holy Spirit; I see the most wondrous way to lead a new life for Christ. I wish my life in today's time was as rewarding as it was with them. I must each day start my life anew with the Spirits help. I'm sure they did too but in today's world Faith is not as strong as it was then; I believe but I don't think I can move a mountain? The Apostles removed demons, brought back to life and healed many of God's children. They were truly filled with the Holy Spirit of God. That is the type of Spirit I wish for to fill my life; I strive each and every day to do Gods bidding with all my heart.

This brings me to the words in (1 Thessalonians 5-19) "do not quench the Spirit." I fell at times I'm opposing the Spirits work in me, I must not forget that I have received the word of the Gospel and my Faith must be over 100%, with belief in all that I practice. I try to remember this phrase; "if at first you do-not succeed try and try again." I must remember that we can't take a lackadaisical attitude of what we can and cannot do with the help of the Holy Spirit and the Gifts of the Spirit. I should consider that this is a warning to me and I need to put my Faith where my heart leads me! I must give the Holy Spirit more room in my heart and listen to what He says and shows me. I need to use the gift of Patience. Faithfulness and self- control more appropriately in order to achieve my faith in moving the mountain that is in front of me.

Pontius Pilate remarked "what is the truth" this was in answer to what Jesus had said, John 19:36-38, (paraphrased). "I tell you the truth my kingdom is not of this world, but now my kingdom is of another world; I am a king, I was born into this world that I would testify to the truth; and anyone who believes in the truth listens to me." As power of authority goes Jesus should have been able to use soldiers to control any and all situations. But His was not of military might was it? He came to make us all aware of the Truth of the Gospel of God!

I would like to make know to you how we can see the truth looking into the Word of God.

The first verse is from John 17-17, "Sanctify them in the Truth; Your Word is Truth". I see Jacob the son of Isaac, grand-son of Abraham, who has been given a renewing of the covenant given to Abraham; that leads his family tree right to King David and then to Jesus Lord and Messiah.

The second verse is from John 8-32, "and you will know the Truth and the Truth will set you free." We must be ready to give a defensive accounting of the word of God, and that of Jesus who taught us of those things of God and that the Holy Spirit is here to bring reverence to the Truth that Jesus spoke off.

In Genesis 35- 9-12, God appeared to Jacob and changed his name to Israel; God said to him; I am God Almighty; be fruitful and multiply; many nations and Kings will come from you. The land I gave to Abraham and Isaac I give to you; and to all your descendants. Some facts about Jacob; his name change was given to the land of the Israelites; he was the founding father of Israel; king David and Solomon both reigned over Israel. The monarchy was divided up in the north was Israel, and to the south was Judah. On the return from the eviction to Babylon the nation was one again called Israel! From Jacob came the twelve tribes of Israel; as they are known today in the Book of Revelations: 7:5-7. We find Asher, Benjamin, Gad, Joseph, Judah, Issachar, Levi, Manasseh, Naphtali, Ruben, Simeon, Zebulon. The Genealogy of Abraham to Salmon can be seen in Matthew 1: 1-4; I would like to skip ahead in time to Salmon the father of Boaz and his wife Ruth. To them was born O'bed father of Jesse, who was born to him his son David. From David was born Solomon and from the house of Solomon; this was the tree line of Joseph and his wife Mary who begat Jesus born from the Union of the Holy Spirit of God.

We are able to seek the Truth when we learn what is in the Gospel of Gods, Old Testament, and His Sons New Testament. I find love from the Book of God as I put it in perspective of a story; which is worthwhile telling to all who are willing to learn the Truth about the word of God.

7

GIVING SERVICE OF GLORY

g. The Holy Spirit of God acts for me in every way and manner possible to assist me in speaking to Almighty God! This is done not only for me but also for my Church brethren, those in my State and all of the United States, even the whole World? When we make a confession of faith, sin, repentance, and a promises to do good unto all we do! It is the Holy Spirit who is right there just as God is all about omnipresence, so is His Holy Spirit.

In Isaiah 63; we find that Isaiah is praying to God to once more please show your kindness to your people! He says that the people of God are in distress, and realize the wrong they have done; as they did in the days of coming across the desert of Egypt. He has asked God to look down from Heaven once again and show His Glorious zeal for His people. In Verse 17' "Why oh Lord do you make us wander from your ways and harden our hearts? Isaiah asks where you are Lord who has spared His children from the Red Sea, and shepherd them in safety; and (V-11) "where is he who set His Holy Spirit among them. (V-12) "Who sent His glorious Arm of power to be at Moses right hand to divide the waters before them?"

Isaiah wants God's Glory of the Holy Spirit to return to Israel His people, once again.

Gods Glory, His Holy Spirit is available to us today, as we would ask of Him to be with us in all we do. We can be brought out of the bondage of sin and decay; as the Holy Spirit formed the Earth in the beginning of Creation with all the power of God, He can perform upon us a freedom that will set us free. In Romans 8:21, "That the creation itself will be liberated from its bondage to decay' and brought into the freedom and the Glory of the children of God." We will be renewed in a Glorified spiritual body, just as the earth will be renewed and not destroyed (Revelations 21-1), " and I saw a new Heaven descend on a new Earth." all living things will not be subject to dying as we do today in this earthly body. Our Universe is not destined for destruction but a makeover as we are.

The service of Glory that most people see or take part in is different than the Glory of the Holy Spirit. For instance my wife and I have been able to see, (7) seven accomplishments we fell proud of. We have been on all (7) continents, we got to view some of the greatest mountains of the world; but more important to us, we saw some of the oldest Churches on those continents. Then I realized that when I walk through a cemetery and see any of the symbols of grave stones, the Cross, or even military symbols of firearms. I think of those men and women serving in the Military, Police officers, or Firefighters; that gave of themselves that others might see their own accomplishments of their goals in life; like mine! They gave their lives so we might have an abundance of some of the benefits of a stable life; as most of us force it! I'm also reminded of the only one who gave His life that we may have an abundance of the Eternal Life promised to each of us who accept Jesus; this then lets God the Father know to bring Glory to Jesus, His Son. The life that Christ Jesus gave up for us and our sins was not the only Glory that we received; He also gave us the opportunity to receive the Glory of God through His Holy Spirit! We all need to set tangible goals for our spiritual lives; especially when we receive the Glory of the Holy Spirit; and as He comes into our hearts. When you do this and you feel Him tugging at your heart and your mind; He reminds you to realize that your goals have been met! (Isaiah 60:1), "Arise, shine; for your light has come, the Glory of the Lord has risen upon you."

You may not be able to see the Holy Spirit now; but with great faith we believe that He is present; we may have inexpressible thoughts and words; He is still able to let His Glory shine through any dark clouds!

Remember this from John 17-22, "The Glory which you have given me I have given to them, that they may be one, just as you and I are one."

Our dreams of the Eternal Life are secure as we come face to face with the teaching and comfort of the Holy Spirit. Each morning we pray for a better day and a safer day with confidence, that His Spirit is with us, just look into the mirror you should be able to realize that you are filled with the Glory of the Holy Spirit and are ready to go forth and transform someone else's life for the sake and Glory of Jesus.

When we accept the Ministry of the Holy Spirit we bring Glory to Jesus; therefore the Holy Spirit is the source of our Glory to Jesus that brings a righteousness of all those things we do through the Spirit! The original Ministry of the Spirit came to use through Moses, when he received the Law by the way of the Tablets! These engraved tablets of stone came with the shining Glory of the Spirit as it appeared on Moses face. The people were afraid to look at Moses because the Glory of God gave a blinding light; they could not stand to look at. Today's ministry is based on how we use the Spirit to make our righteousness to be the Glorious exchange of the teaching of wisdom from the Holy Spirit. The tablets of the Ten Laws of the Old Covenant are not to be said they were bad or evil; they certainly have their place in this world even today. They actually out-lined all the positive things we need to do and give us what the punishment could be indirectly for not keeping them.

2 Corinthians 3: 9-10, "If the ministry that brought condemnation was glorious, how much more glorious is the ministry that brings a righteousness! For what was glorious has no glory now in comparison with the surpassing glory." The original Ten laws brought on death when they were broken; no one could keep them; break one and you break them all! Today the Spirit reminds us that Jesus died on the cross for our sins and we need but ask for forgiveness and repent to lead a better life free from sin.

AS HE IS ABLE TO GIVE US LIFE

We do not see the Holy Spirit of God but He is real; we love Him; and because of this love we believe in Him, we can rejoice with the greatest of feeling of joy and we will be filled with His Glory.

(Verse 3:18) "But we all, with unveiled face, beholding as in a mirror the Glory of the Lord, are being transformed into the same image from Glory to Glory, just as from the Lord, the Holy Spirit."

Moses put the Vail on for two reasons; one to stop the people from being afraid, and so the people would not see the fading brightness of the Glory of the Spirit that was on him!

CHAPTER 6   SUMMARY
GIVING LIVES

We have found that living a spirit found life is just what God wants us to be able to commit to. The Holy Spirit gives us many chances to give and to share that gift with those who may need it. Our lives are predicated on each breath we take! Our heart ensures us with each beat we get that breath! Life for all was initially formed, when God took dirt in his hand and formed mankind. Then from the bone of man God formed woman. They both in turn were given the fruitful ability to form new life together, as one. The Holy Spirit reminds us we as a family man and woman can lead spiritual filled lives here is this world today!

I have selected Seven Ways to show you as to how the Holy Spirit is giving to us ability to leading a Godly life here on Earth.

a.   In living a spiritually filled life, I looked at Job, Sampson, Jesus and His Apostles. Each of them in turn showed us that their use of the knowledge given to them was brought about in their ability of how they were able to display great wisdom in all their actions; of strength and faith in the life they had lead. Thank God that they actually shared all that was given to them, as in miracles of faith, the writing of the New Testament and teaching disciples that were willing to follow the Way of Christ.

As a parent I was expected to share in the raising of our children;

setting an example was and is still a factor today as always! My behavior was seen by my children and they watched everything I did and your children do likewise. We can set good and bad examples for them to follow! If we claim that we are led by the Holy Spirit of God then we should act as we say that we do. .

In the Book of Act's I have found that the Holy Spirit's presence acting in the spirit of each of the Apostles was phenomenal; the Spirit was with them 24/7 as they went about evangelizing the His death on the cross and His resurrection and accentuation to the Right Hand of God. Remember this we must ask the Holy Spirit to come and live in our hearts He will then remind us of all those things Jesus taught us, to share to all by giving to those that would listen to the words of His teaching.

b.   Remember the phrase, "Except for the Grace of God there go I". The Holy Spirit resides within us; we are all capable of determining goodness from evilness! This comes about because we believe in the Gospel of Jesus; that the Spirit convicts us of what is needed to lead a life worthy of the Grace of God. Jesus insured our salvation when he died on the Cross as the faithful Son of God. He was resurrected to show us He is alive and He sits at the Right Hand of God. When we sin, we ask for forgiveness, and it is because of the Grace of God we will be forgiven. Every time we find ourselves in a situation and feel we cannot get out of it we need to remember the (W.W.J.D.); just what would Jesus do? After all Jesus is the Greatest Teacher/Prophet we have ever know who came from God the Father Almighty.

We must also take into account that it is Gods Laws that we need to uphold; not the man created laws that will take us away from our Faith that keeps us in touch with God. We must also be careful of those words coming from the pulpit, bible classes or bible studies; the wrong interpretation or even the lack of teaching all there is in the Bible; like the creation, Birth of Jesus and how it came about, plus His death and the fact He did ascend to be with Father God. We saw that all those who control our lives through the Laws of the land cannot make themselves above reproach of the Laws they are asked to enforce.

Search your hearts and mind for the gifts that God has predestined for you to have and share it with the body of your church. It is by His grace that you will be saved; because of the sacrifice that Christ made for us to receive the life sustaining Salvation that will led us home to Heaven.

c.   I remember each time my wife, children and I had to move; about every eighteen months (as we were in the Air Force for twenty years). It was very hard for all of us meeting new people, starting new jobs, and new schools; new neighbors and new Churches. The one place that made it better was at the Church, they accepted us as if we were old friends we became their Adopted family in Christ our Lord. I have heard many people say it was like hell getting started again; things were not very easy! I always asked what Church did you come from and where did you attend church when you arrived at your new destination? Oh! I really didn't look for one as I was too busy getting settled in. Church was not on my mind at that time! You didn't pray about your situation before leaving or when you arrived at your new home? I found this In the Book of Isaiah!

In Isaiah 48:17 The Lord God had this to say, "I am the Lord your God, who teaches you what is best for you, who directs you in the way you should go." You looking to a better welcoming each time you move around; you want to be part of the Family of God! Then send everything to Him in prayer, asks the Holy Spirit to lead you in every direction you are going. Once you have been adopted into the Family of God you are there for the life of your faith. Abrahams covenant from God assures us of an Adoption Pass to receive all the benefits that God promised to him would be passed on from one generation to the present day generation! We are all the children of God and we are all a part of the Family of God; Amen.

d.   God has predestined each of us to be Holy; Jesus will find you and you will then be convicted by the Holy Spirit of God. He will make you an exclusive person as seen in John 15-16 this is done because He Jesus has chosen you to be Holy and righteous through the knowledge of the word of God. Paul and all the other Apostles said, "We have come as servants of our Lord Christ Jesus; we should do likewise". When we call upon others to come to Christ we should do it in the name of The Father and of The Son and of The Holy Spirit. Remember this verse from 1 Peter 1: 15-16, "But like the Holy One that called you, be Holy yourselves also in all your behavior; because it is written, you shall be Holy because I am Holy."

e.   Where or who do we go to for problem solving? We go to the Holy Spirit of God and it is through our Prayers of Supplication that we will make our request, and get our answers. We were to put on the Armor of Protection of the Holy Spirit as outlined in Chapter 5. Then I gave a Seven Steps;

1.   Remember Him on a daily basis.

2.   Keep Holy a Day of Worship.

3.   He has your back (or Six) ever since the creation.

4.   Praise Him; give Him a Thank you' and bless Him for everything He has given you.

5.   Remember the phone number for Him is (2 Sam! 22-4)

6.   Position for prayer is whatever way you feel comfortable to Praise Him.

7.   "Remember to extol His works which men have praised in song." (Job 36-4) May we all find a Peace in all our Payers of Supplication?

f.   Then there was the word "Truth"; Pontius Pilate made this statement; "Truth what is the Truth". Then Jesus answered him with this; "I tell you the Truth My Kingdom is not of this world, but now My Kingdom is of another world, and I am a King; I was born into this world to testify to the Truth, and anyone who listens to me believes in me." We are required to pass on the Holy Word of God, and we are not to quench the Holy Spirit in doing so. We must believe and have great faith in the teaching of Jesus the Christ. We are then able to seek the Truth when we learn what is in the Gospel of God's Old Testament, and that of Jesus's New Testament; here we find the Truth from Gods creation to the Revelation of the future.

g.   The Holy Spirit of God teaches us how to give Services of Glory not only to God but to one another! Whenever I visit another country I look for the Cemetery of our fallen servicemen whose bodies were not brought home to be buried; I think of what they sacrificed for God and Country. They fought for the freedom and rights of others in a faraway land; because that's the dream we embellish for one another in America. Whenever servicemen went out on patrol with a squad; they prayed a prayer that God's Glory would be with them and that they be protected in doing the righteous acts that were necessary, to complete the mission!

As you travel the narrow path to God's Glory may you do justice in all your actions? We may not be able to physically see the Holy Spirit; but He is there and with great faith we will feel His presence.

I look forward to bringing Glory to Jesus, and I do that by accepting the Ministry of the Holy Spirit. It is by our actions that we can bring Glory to Jesus and we only have to remember Moses he came down from the mountain each time his face was shining ever so brightly he had to cover up the Glory of the Spirit of God so as not to frighten the people when they looked at him. Let our Glory shine in our actions.

A QUEST FOR BENEFITS

THE SEVENTH OF
SEVEN STEPS

Chapter 7

---∾---

Our QUEST of Using HIS Benefits

If the lord said to you; I know a man that knows a man, who knows of a man that can help you no matter what it is? How would you react to this? In Acts 18: 9-10; we find a statement very similar to that saying. "And the Lord said to Paul in the night by a vision, "Do not be afraid any longer, but go on speaking and do not be silent; for I am with you, and no man will attack you in order to harm you, for I have many people in this city." God gives us ways out of any situation all we have to do is to call upon the Holy Spirit to guide us in all matters! We must have faith and trust in God.

I found in Job 31: 24-28; he was lamenting to his friends about trusting in God; Para-phrased: If I put my trust in God and called it security? Or if I have rejoiced over my wealth and great fortune that I have gained! If I have regarded the sun and the moon in its radiance; so that my heart was secretly enticed and I blew kisses of courage with my hands up to them; I would be judged by God as a sinner and as unfaithful unto Him!

Job put his faith in Gods Holy Spirit for his future, in spite of the suffering he endured. He knew that God would raise him from his trials, no matter how hard they were at the moment. The knowledge of the Holy Spirit comes to us in trusting in Him at all times.

In God We Trust is stamped on all of our monies in America. Then there are the politicians giving us rhetoric in assuring us that the Senior citizens of Americas Social Security system stands strong; we should not sweat it; the retirement system is safe, such as can be? We as Americans are told to plan for the future. There are many obstacles that can be placed in our way; some not proven to be safe, or even sound reliable. Let me offer you this; If Jesus was to ask you this one question! Are you thinking of the future! The Holy Spirit is hiring right now; you can work for God and the Retirement system and its Benefits are out of this World. As I conclude this last Chapter, of Seven Steps Seven Ways; the Holy Spirit who is the Greatest Servant of God; let me remind you of His purpose!

The Holy Spirit is the Advocate that Jesus promised all who believe that Jesus is the Son of God. He is the Spirit of Truth; He is God's Spirit. He will testify to all things Jesus taught and those things of God from the beginning of time that God has written on our hearts. We also need to live with the expectations that Jesus is coming soon. In the 1st century the Christians believed that whole heartedly; they gave to one another all their possessions to be shared, they gave their love to one another as Jesus suggested they should "love one another as they would love themselves." They went from house to house, city to city, and Temple to Temple preaching the Good News of Jesus Birth, Death and His resurrection. There was this Teacher of the Temple that came to Jesus only at night time, he would come to talk to Jesus; on this particular night he called out to Jesus and said, "Rabbi we know that you have come from God, no man can teach the way you teach. Rabbi the miracles that you perform can only be that of Gods way. Jesus then answered Nicodemus, "Truly I say to you, no one can come into the kingdom of God unless he is born again. This was startling to Nicodemus; he said how can an Old Man go back into his mother's womb? Jesus replied, "Unless you are born of the water and of the Spirit no one can enter into the Kingdom of God! This statement is for all who have been born in this world as God has given

His Spirit to all. It is up to each one to accept Jesus as the Son of God; Gods reward comes in His saying in John 3-16; "For God so loved the world, He gave His only Son, and those who believe in Him shall not perish, but have everlasting life."

There is a sure way to the Kingdom of God and that is found in John 14-6, "I am the Way the Truth and the Life; no one shall come unto the Father unless it is by me" (Jesus). Once again it is the Advocate promised by Jesus who convicts us of all truths said by Jesus, that He is the Son of God and the Holy Spirit resides in us and holds us to these Truths. All we have to do is call upon the Holy Spirit and He will insure us that all things are possible with Gods Spirit working in our hearts. There are not many guarantees out there, so work on this one!

I have picked the following Seven Ways of the Benefits of the Holy Spirit. These are the ways we can benefit from His Knowledge, Wisdom, Faith, Healing, Miracle's, Prophecy's and the Seeing of Spirits.

Jesus is coming soon and we need to be prepared! In the book of Revelations 21-1, John tells us this in 10 words or less; also in Genesis 1-1 we find this;

"I saw a new Heaven descending on a new Earth." This is a reflection of how the beginning began, and how it will end. "In the beginning God created the Heavens and the Earth." The Kingdom of God is going to be remade for all those who believe that Jesus is the Son of God and He is coming soon. Amen.

a.   The first of the seven ways will be Knowledge as only the Holy Spirit can give it to us. This understanding is gained from experiences of all the information that is stored in us, or otherwise learned from the Spirit of our Heart; and even doing good works pleasing to God.

b.   The second is that of Wisdom, how we can function with all that has been given to us. It is the accumulation of all things learned by using good common sense. In the Bible, Solomon is considered the man of great wisdom for mankind to follow; this was up to the time he decided to follow a path in the lusting of women.

c.   The Third way of His benefits is that of Faith, there are two meanings of faith. The 1ˢᵗ is how we can use it like in keeping a promises or believing that it will happen. The 2ⁿᵈ knowing when we trust in something or someone and it is a reliable source of information; we will have faith in a good conclusion. We have faith that God will keep His promises as we have seen in His Covenants with mankind. Faith is the foundation of our religious beliefs!

d. The Fourth is in Healing; the dictionary tells us it is the renewing of any broken bones we may get on our bodies; we will need some time to heal. When Healing is complete we will be considered as made whole again!

Eve and Adam sinned in the Garden of God; they created the original sin that all of mankind would bear with fear of Hell and Damnation, but God, wasn't happy He wanted us healed from sin, so He sent His only Son to us and those who believed in Him would be free from sin. (Our Baptism will protect us from the original sin along with other pledges to God)

e.   The Fifth way is that of the use of the Miraculous Powers as Jesus used them. And of God's Grace. Miracles are signs of a divine intervention. I have to tell you I'm jealous of the 1ˢᵗ Century Saints! They were truly filed with the Holy Spirit as they were able to go out and perform Miracles on those that needed healing! It is disturbing to me that my faith and the faith of others cannot perform those types of Miracles? I tell you this though it is by the Grace of God and our Prayers of Supplications that cause the Miracles to happen; the Holy Spirit assures us that our prayers will be answered.

f.   The Sixth way how we can use Prophecy in an evangelistic way. It is a reminder of those things of the future that will come to us. To me it's like a message from God or a warning that we need to hear. It can be about the Past, Present or especially that of the Future. A reminder of the beginning and what Moses wrote, or of the Evangelists today reminding us there is only one way to God and that's through Jesus. Then there is Johns Book of Revelation for our future. I like to think

that people like Billy Graham can be like a Prophet when they evangelize that Jesus is coming soon.

g.   The Seventh way is how we look at what is within us for the signs of
His Spiritual gifts. I believe that there is a space around us where spirits
are living in an unseen world. We can't see them; there are good and bad
spirits all around us; But that is not what the Holy Spirit is all about; you
see, He has gifts for us that we can practice at in order to lead a fulfilling
life in order to perform a service to the Church. There is a ministry of
blessed ones teaching and guiding us to lead a religious life. There are
those gifts, which lead us to help others with their walk in life for Christ.
    These Fruitful Gifts will enhance the Gifts of the Spirit like putting
Icing on a Cake! They will bring out the true delightfulness of what
I'm talking about, the Fruit of the Spirit; Love, Joy, Peace, Patients,
Faithfulness, Goodness, Gentleness, Kindness, and Self Control. This
is to be our path in life filled with the Holy Spirit of God.
    A Life without Christ and who He represents guided by the Holy
Spirit; was visible with a lot of service men in combat; being a retired
military man I have seen the eyes of the dying and witnessed the en-
trails of war. This depiction of being a man without a cause or understanding of what our creator wanted us to do; the following quote may
fit? A Quote from the Man from La Mancha!

> *"Life as it is; I've lived for over 40 years and I've seen life as it
> is Pain, Misery, and Cruelty all beyond belief. I've heard all the
> voices of God's noblest creature. Then moans from the bundles of
> filth found in the street. I've been a soldier and a slave. I've seen
> my comrade's fall in battle or die more slowly under the lash in
> Africa. I've held them in my arms at the final moment. These were
> men who saw life as it is, yet they died despairing. No glory, no
> brave last words, only their eyes, filled with confusion, questioning
> "Why?" I don't think they were asking why they were dying, but
> why they had ever lived. When life itself seems lunatic, who knows
> where madness lies? Perhaps to be too practical is madness to sur-
> render dreams - -this may be madness; to seek treasure where there*

is only trash. Too much sanity may be madness! And maddest of all - to see life as it is and not, as it should be!"

We need the Holy Spirit to give to us more information; seek first God's answer as to how we can lead a respectable life, one that would honor Him, one that you may serve Him as we are His children; He wants nothing but the best for us!

1

TREE OF KNOWLEDGE

a.   Our source for knowledge is without a doubt is God Almighty; who invites us to also look to Jesus, the Holy Spirit, and the World that we live in; this will give us added insight in our Quest for the Benefit of Knowledge!

There is some knowledge gained that causes us (Mankind) in general to sin, seek out things that can tempt us like lusting in our own desires! Knowledge knowing who God is and what He wants us to do by His will. We are required to seek out His Son Jesus, we need to learn how to pray so that we can talk to God and receive the Blessing of His knowledge from the Holy Spirit as we ask in Supplication.

The knowledge of the Holy Spirit is no different than that of God the Father Almighty! He is all knowing and His knowledge goes back before any time we can think of? Before we were even born He knew what would be inside of us and what our needs would be. The Holy Spirit cannot be caught off guard, He reads us through the feelings of our heart. He notices all who ask for help seeking to do good unto all mankind that we might Love one another as God loves us.

In 1 Corinthian 2: Paul stated, "He did not come in eloquence or in wisdom" but he came with the knowledge of the testimony of Christ Jesus and Him crucified! Paul felt at this time he may not be able to give them enough knowledge to satisfy them that Christ lives. Paul resolved himself that he would teach and preach nothing but the message of Christ Jesus. Paul wasn't about to teach to the people of Corinth with fancy words and any teacher or preacher today's must recognize this and make it simple enough that a child may understand the message. Paul taught with great knowledge; his training and schooling as a Roman citizen and a Jewish Pharisee gained him this great knowledge! We can see here that unless the Holy Spirit is working in the hearts of all receivers of His message it cannot be effective.

"Paul did not use wise and persuasive words but with a demonstration of the Spirits Power." He did this through the healing of the sick and the maimed! He was seeking to convince them that this power was also available to them by seeking Jesus as the Son of God and through the repentance of sin and being Baptized and asking for the Holy Spirit to fill their lives.

Paul also revealed to them a mystery that has been hidden from them ever since the beginning of time, by God. It was also noted that, had anyone in authority new of the hidden messages they would not have crucified Lord Jesus. Verse 9, tells us this "What no eye has seen, what no ear has heard, and what no human mind has conceived" those things of God has prepared for those who love Him. We should not think that this is limited to the past or the present but the future of all blessing as well. The Holy Spirit can and does search all things not that He needs the knowledge; because He is our interpreter and He convicts us of all things because, He does know all things as He is God. In verse 10; "The Spirit searches all things even the Deep things of God."

We must live a life worthy of the Knowledge that we receive from the Word of God. This knowledge along with the Wisdom to use it comes only from the Spirit lead life we are to walk. It is through our thank you to God and prayer's that we are able to converse with God the Father

Almighty. We as humans should not have to be thanked for our Faith and love , we need to thank God who is the source of the virtues of Jesus, His Son, and for the Holy Spirit of God who ensures we will receive all we ask for from the bottom of our, hearts. Paul says for this reason we have not stopped praying for all of you we will continually ask God to fill you with the Knowledge of His will. (Paraphrased) Colossians 1: 3-9

All of His knowledge is coupled together with our Faith, Hope and love for His Holy Word which is the way He talks to us and we talk to Him through our prayers. We must continue to spread the Word of the Gospel. Whenever I look at the first day of Pentecost the Holy Spirit has been made available to all who seek his Son Jesus and ask for God's Holy Spirit.

The Holy Spirit intercedes for us in our (Quest) in a way of pleading our case before God Almighty, Paul said, "In the same way, the Spirit helps us in our weakness. We do not know what we ought to pray for, but the Spirit Himself intercedes for us with groans that words cannot express." Do you want the very best Lawyer for your case to be heard before the Almighty then get in touch with the Holy Spirit to plead your case!

(John 16: 8-9) Jesus said, "When he comes the Holy Spirit will convict the World of guilt in the regard to sin and righteousness and judgment; In regard to sin, because mankind does not believe in me."

Gods ultimate use for us is that of our Sanctification unto Him, and that process has to come through the Holy Spirit; as He gives us knowledge of not only His Gifts, but by exhibiting the divine Gifts of the Fruit of the Spirit; adding quality and enhancing the attributes of our personalities.

Remember this that the Word of Knowledge, is the Holy Spirit is trying to fill us with His special source of Knowledge that we don't have the ability or the means to receive; as we are limited in the levels of intelligence and that of knowledge. Think of it as a supernatural experience given only by the Holy Spirit, and not by our own mind which lacks the intelligence to conceive it.

I believe that the Holy Spirit actually manifest this Gift of knowledge a lot more than we can realize, and we actually fail to see it when it does come our way in life? Basically it is because they that believe have not been taught the Spirit can do this for them. Use the Spirit for this life saving gift of Knowledge for any of life's problems we may come-upon.

Some of today's problems can be fixed with the use of the Fruits of the Spirit, the love, joy, patience; attitude can help to persuade those we are counseling.

KNOWLEDGE, IS ASKING FOR HELP AS IN THE FOLLOWING EXAMPLES;

1. Helping students to solve a math problem at school.
2. Solving a specific problem at your work place.
3. Where you may have misplaced your car keys at.
4. How we can apply to our own personal life what a certain Scripture verse may mean.
5. Witnessing to an unsaved family member.
6. How we can intercede in a marital dispute.
7. Starting up a new business. As you can see from these kinds of examples, there is literally nothing that the Holy Spirit cannot get into in your own personal life where He can then give you a word of knowledge on how to properly handle something that you are currently dealing with, or give you a word of knowledge to help someone else out with what they may be dealing with on their end.

2

WISDOM

b. Isaiah 11: 2, "The Spirit of the Lord will rest upon him, the Spirit of Wisdom and of understanding; the Spirit of counsel and of might;

the Spirit of knowledge and fear of the lord." The Gift of Wisdom is the Wisdom of God. It comes to us in a supernatural way, that of the Holy Spirit who reads those things of God written on our hearts. Found in (Ephesians 1-17).

There is a story of a woman named Lydia; she was a dealer in tenting material which was of interest to Paul. How it came about was from a dream that Paul had (Acts 16-9-15) in this dream he saw a man from Macedonia standing and begging him to come and help him? What I see here is Paul asked that he be given visions of what he can do and where he should go to accomplish the Lords work. In other words ask and you will receive of the Holy Spirit's Wisdom to go forth and Minister to those who are in need! When Paul arrived there he preached to a crowd, and in the crowd was this woman Lydia from Thyatira, and her whole household was present and they accepted Jesus and were baptized. She was a woman of God to begin with, but she needed the words of wisdom of the Cross to assure her that her faith would be confirmed as God had written on her heart.

The Holy Spirit gives to all who are called to speak to solve problems and who are in need of coming up with solutions. All we have to do is ask the Lord to fill us with wisdom and the understanding of which can open doors to accomplish the Lords work. We find this gift works well with the gifts of knowledge and that of discerning of the Spirits. It also gives us an insight of divine direction in our being led by the Holy Spirit.

The Holy Spirit is the embodiment of Godly Wisdom to be understood by those who call upon Him for help. We need to ask the Lord to fill us in, so we may see His power of applying true wisdom to every situation.

1. See how the Spirit Looks at Wisdom to Imitate Godly Love.

2. Let us see how the Spirit gives us Directions of leadership.

3. See how the Spirit Gives Wisdom to those who speak of Godly things.

4. See how He Illuminates the Wisdom found in Christ.

5. Let the Spirit take the Lead listen to Him.

6. Watch for the Signs of how He can Deliver and Protect.

7. Let Him reveal to you the Wisdom of the Cross.

In seeking Wisdom we find three areas of Wisdom. The first is that Wisdom that comes from the mysteries of God, and His secrets hidden from us! This is the way we use the wisdom of the knowledge that He has given to us through the Power of Holy Spirit; 1 Corinthians 2-7 that is found written on our hearts and that is gained from the reading of the Word of God.

Before Christ our Lord was crucified on the cross, God had not revealed His mystery's to the extent that man could understand them. Mankind with all his wisdom or even through his power of reasoning was not able to understand the meaning of the cross and if they had been able to do so they may not have crucified Him. The message of the cross took on a different meaning for those who were suffering? The way of the cross was foolishness to them. Human reasoning caused them to see things in a different supernatural level! They exalted and sought out a form of human wisdom with human deductions for their answers.

In 1 Corinthians 1-18 tells us this "the way of the cross is foolishness to those who are suffering; those who believe it is the way to eternal life".

The second is that of the Natural World? Those gifts of Wisdom, that the world offers us through the experiences that we share with one another; and of our talents that God has given to each of us.

1 Corinthians 2-6.

It is said at times when those who feel left out and do not understand the situation they are in; they ignore all there is in the meaning of the cross.

I don't believe in a heaven or a hell! I was once told this by a friend of mine; He also said, "When we die our bodies just rot away in the grave?" Wow that doesn't say much for the most sophisticated living thing in this universe. I asked how he was born, was he hatched from something, was he the drippings of someone's sweat or maybe the rain drops fell on good grass and he was formed. When people think that life is nothing and they are so inbred with the wisdom of this world; like schools of knowledge and they receive Doctors degrees of education! They actually feel they know more than anyone and can make observations, like we don't know anything! We as Christian are who believe in the message of the cross, find that Gods wisdom is greater than any human wisdom gained in this world. After all we as Christians have promises that there is more to the empty grave of ashes, there is eternal life with the creator of the most sophisticated living thing in Gods universe, and the Holy Spirit will convict us of all of Gods secrets when we need them!

The third is that of mankind? As our Christian association with one another, sharing our beliefs and keeping His word in the practice of attending Bible schools and Bible lesson at Church or in some-one's home. We have been commissioned to do as the Apostles and Disciples of the 1st Century have been commissioned to do; that is to preach and baptize in the name of the Father and of the Son and of the Spirit. Acts 6: 1-10. We find that the responsibility that the Apostles were to take on of their feeding and caring for the needy and the poor and the widows was a little over whelming. The number of disciples was increasing as the Church grew the problem grew of helping them rather than Preaching. We find that this 1st Century Church problems were strictly Jewish in nature? There were the Hellenistic Jews those that were born in other lands outside of the Israel Holy Lands! They spoke in tongues of Greek more than that of the Hebraic Jews language of Hebrew Aramaic.

Wisdom is being given the right tools to be of special service to God! In Exodus 31-3 we find this statement meant for a man named Bezalel, God said, "I have filled him with the Spirit of God and that of Wisdom, with understanding, with knowledge, and with all kinds of skills." This man was an artist of Gods designing to build and enhance that of Gods Tent of Meetings. He would be able to discern perfectly the mind of Gods heart and of those things God wanted done or could have done to Him; but instead He chose this man Bezalel, so that we can know that when we call upon the Lord He will send the Holy Spirit to fill us with knowledge and the wisdom to use it. Let us have confidence in what and how the Holy Spirit makes those things that are the mysteries and secrets of what God has put in our hearts and minds come true! The Holy Spirit will actually search and separate any and all things that are in a contradictory nature to what God wants us to know.

We cannot conceive God through the eyes of man's world! God has made foolish the wisdom of the world and for those who try to find out who He is. The only way to understand who God is; is through His Son Jesus. The Holy Spirit is here in a supernatural way to convict us of the true meaning of the cross!

The cross is the expression of the divine wisdom of God insuring us of His love and humility. After all it was God that died on that cross for our sins. He came in the form of man; imbedded in the womb of a virgin, and He assumed the name of the only one that could possible give us saving grace; to enter into the kingdom of God. God said this about the Son He created; "This is my Son, whom I love; with Him I am well pleased." (Matthew 3-17). Then God said at the mount of Transfiguration; "This is my Son, whom I love; with Him I am well pleased. Listen to Him." (Verse 17-5)

We must have confidence in the fact that the Holy Spirit teaches us of the spiritual things of God. We don't know what others are thinking but the Spirit of God does; so let us call upon Him to fill us with the Wisdom of God; in order for us to accomplish our gifts of the Spirit.

3

FAITH

c. What we are is a body designed of flesh and bones; what we wish to be is a body without pain and suffering; one that is a body of spiritual means. Are you ready to make the jump across the big chasm of life's problems? Our Faith ensures us of a life eternal in Gods Heaven! This is because of His Son Jesus; and those things of Gods Holy Spirit that convicts us of all things God and Jesus have been made known to us to be true. Here are seven thoughts to pounder on.

1. We can see Faith in ways other than a saving faith.

2. Looking at faith differently other than faithfulness.

3. Seeing the faith in moving a mountain.

4. Faith that is exhibited by the heroes of the Bible.

5. Giving as the words of wisdom are given to enhance our minds.

6. As God wants to communicate with us.

7. Believing that His Spirit is being poured over us.

Our faith is expressed in the power of the Holy Spirit to carry out all kinds of ministries in order for us to serve God. Jesus wants us to go forth and make disciples of all nations, we do this because we have faith in what we are taught by Jesus and convicted by the Holy Spirit, of Gods Gospel!

In the 1st Century, the Apostles taught that God accepts people by their Faith; whether they are Jewish or Gentile. They made it clear that any who believed in Christ should not be burdened with obligations that the Jewish people were forced to TRY and keep holy! There were those Pharisee believers that the standard of circumcision and the Laws of Moses needed to be kept. Of course this would undermine the reason that Christ Jesus died on the cross! Peter himself in Acts 15:10-11; that those who attempted to be saved by obeying the Laws was actually, "a yoke hanging on the necks of those." coming to Christ. They did not need to embrace the Law; "but the grace of the Lord Jesus, was the way to be saved."

In Acts 10-11; Peter took a leap of Faith! He realized that God does not show partiality when people accept Him as Lord of all. Especially those who want to know more about our Savior and Messiah. There was this Sergeant Major Cornelius; who was Commander of a Regiment of Italians; who was God fearing men! Cornelius had been converted to Judaism and did believe in the concept of a one God religion!

He respected the morals and ethical teachings of the Jewish people he gave to those who were in need and prayed daily. He wanted to know more especially about a man named Jesus of Nazareth! "One evening while in prayer, an Angel of the Lord came to him in a vision; Cornelius stared at him in fear, and asked what it was that he could do for his Lord? The Angel said your prayers have been answered and your gifts to the poor have come before God. You are to send men to Joppa to bring back a man named Simon called Peter, staying at the house of Simon the Tanner." When the angel left he called two of his servants and a devout soldier and told them of his vision and what they were to do. Almost at the same time Peter was having a dream while he waited for his food to be cooked. This dream was uncanny. "There was a blanket being let down from heaven above with four footed animals as well as reptiles and birds lying on the blanket.

"A voice told him; (voice of God) gets up Peter kill and eat." This happened three times; Peter said, "Surely not Lord, Lord I have never eaten anything impure or unclean." God told him, "Do not call anything impure that God has made clean."

As Peter wondered about the dream the men from Cornelius had arrived; the Angel said to Peter, "Simon there are three men downstairs looking for you, do not hesitate to go with them." Peter went down to great them. They told him of the story that Cornelius had in a vision from the Lord. The next day Peter went with them to Caesarea. Cornelius needed to hear the story of Jesus and the crucifixion and the resurrection. He and his household listened to what Peter had to say and they all were baptized. Peter took on the faith of challenge by entering a house of a non-Jew and an uncircumcised one at that. Then Peter remembered the dream and put two and two together, that God says what is clean and unclean; God does not show favoritism to any race ; those who believe are to be welcomed because of their faith in God. Cornelius needed to receive the message of salvation from the source, Cornelius and his family and his soldiers were all baptized after they heard the story of John the Baptist, how Jesus was anointed with the Holy Spirit, who he ate and drank with, why he was hung on the cross, and his resurrection to be with God the Father. Cornelius faith was proven as the Holy Spirit came upon him and convicted him to seek out more than what was available to him. The meaning of Cornelius dream became clear to him; through faith in Christ we can be declared "clean" by God.

When we put our old life behind us, we realize all that Jesus did in His miracles of healing, His words of telling stories using parables; there is nothing He wouldn't do for you! (If we ask Him) It is by Faith that we believe He is the Almighty, and what He says about himself is true. But if we only look at what He says we shall not believe. It is this, we must be able to see Jesus as He really is that makes us believe, all He has done and said to us. Ask yourself this question? "What do you want Jesus to do for you?"

Remember the words in Luke 18-41; "Lord that I may be able to see again." A man blind from birth was asked by Jesus how I can help you! This man knew that it was Jesus; he was endowed with the power of the Spirit to seek out Jesus, he answered wisely! Do not limit the Lord in doing anything; "Nothing is impossible for God." (Luke 1-37). Have your faith ready to go (keep frosty as my old pastor would say) ask the Lord for anything and He will give it to you by the strength of your own faith He will give to you your heart's desire.

4

HEALING

d. We all get to share in the legacy of Christ Jesus. He reigns at the right hand of God the Father Almighty; all that is His is ours. If my parents were millionaires and they left to all their heirs the sum of $100 dollars; we may feel we didn't get the legacy we expected? But with Jesus He is willing to share His throne with all of those who accept Him as the Son of God the Father Almighty. Our sins have been healed by His shedding of Blood when He hung from the Cross! Jesus tells us the greatest gift we can give to each other is, "To die for one another." (John 15-13)

I remember a story told to me of a family of four, Mom, Dad, Sister and Brother. The sixteen year old sister was diagnosed with a rare blood disease, and required a blood transplant but there were no donors available, except her nine year old brother! Doctors were concerned that he would not be able to understand enough to give his permission to use his blood. The Doctor in charge was elected to ask his permission to use his blood. The Doctor explained that blood was a life-saving fluid for his sister; and he told him about the blood of Jesus! His blood, that saved millions in the whole world before he died, and that his blood could save his sister. So then he was asked for permission to take his blood and give it to his sister!

MY HOLY SPIRIT

Well without any hesitation the boy said yes. The doctor asked why he responded so quickly! He said she is my sister and I love her. As he lay on the operating room table transferring the blood, he fell asleep. When he woke the doctor was right there; the boy asked the doctor when HE was going to Die. Are you ready to give your life for someone in order that they may live a fruitful life in Christ? The Doctor explained to him just how brave he was, and that he was not going to die. The boys sacrifice for his sister is what we need to remember. John 15-13.

"He will wipe away every tear from their eyes. There will be no more death or mourning or crying or even pain for the old order of things has passed away." (Revelation 21:4) Healing is the first step for us when we look to saving a life worthy of Christ's love.

Healing is the ultimate testimony that the Holy Spirit works in you. Speak to Him in prayer, and mediate on the healing you need done. The Word of God is a form of medicine.

1. He is Gods Lord of Healing.

2. He acts as our Medical Doctor.

3. He convicts us that God is the giver of life.

4. He can make us immune to inside and outside threats to our lives.

5. He speaks loudly to you on what your prayerful needs are.

6. He listens while you are meditating seeking guidance and direction.

7. He asks you to go to scripture and seek those that make you comfortable.

Sickness is said to be the work of Satan; we must remember that Jesus defeated him in the desert by quoting scripture; we can use the Holy Spirit to make the devils threats against us become a thing of the past. We know that when we receive pills from the Doctor, he gives specific instructions on the label how we should take it, and how much and the time of day to take it! With God He instructs the Holy Spirit to convict us through our faithfulness, in obeying His Spiritual power; there is only one way to take His medicine and that is from the heart (internally). In Matthew 7:7; we find this "ask and it shall be given to you, seek and you shall find it; knock and it shall be opened unto you!"

In James 5:13, "If there be any among you suffering take it to the Lord in Prayer." You will be given the strength for you to get through any problems that may come to you. (V-14) "Is there anyone happy, let them sing songs of praise." It will be by your faith that these things will be taken care of. This expression of faith is the outward answer from God.

Do you believe in the Positive Power of Prayer? Prayer for Healing increases your Faith in Gods answered prayers especially when they are answered to our satisfaction. Do you want to help someone get healed; well the best medicine is Prayer this is definitely an aid to our faith and the first signs of the healing process brought to us as Gods response to prayer that is offered in faith.

When Jesus sent out the "Twelve in Mark 6:12-13;" Jesus sent them out two by two; each pair to a different village! They were told to take nothing with them I mean nothing (no extra clothes, food, or money) only a staff and the clothes and sandals on their feet. "They went out and preached that people should repent. They drove out many demons and anointed many sick people with oil; and they healed them."

We see the Disciples being sent out on their own, it was the very first mission aided with the power of Jesus and performed as He would have. The message was exactly as Jesus would have given to the people! The oil used was an olive oil with the same mixture as found in the Book of Leviticus.

Did you ever wonder why we have so many Doctors that have specialties? Each of them different or majored in feet, knees, ankles, broken bones of the leg, you get my drift right! The disciples were like that some did better with the lame and some better than others in bringing someone back to life; some in disease's, and there were the ones that could heal anyone of anything. (Acts Chapter- 8)

Any form of healing is the blessing of God; and it enhances the Church as it moves forward.

Do you remember the story of the woman that crawled on the ground to touch the robe of Jesus; she was healed by her faith, Jesus felt the power drain out of Him, He said by your faith woman you have been healed."

(Matthew 9: 21-22) Each of us can produce the power of Healing; if we believe that our Faith does have the correct measure of power.

5

MIRACULOUS – POWERS

e.   What is the Power of the Holy Spirit; the answer my friend may be in the wind! We need to remember this "all things are possible with God." (Luke 1-37) Look at it this way His power is the same as God Almighty; the Holy Spirit is the third person of the Holy Trinity. The Holy Spirit can enable us with Miraculous Power; power that can help us be better servants of God. We must be careful that there is nothing blocking our receiving the baptism of the Spirit.

The power of the Spirit does come through a United Church; one that prays together, and stays united with each other! If you should feel there is something blocking your receiving the Spirit of God, you need to pray over it together. So I say this; the power of God comes through the Holy Spirit of God; and the power shall be according to your Faith. The greater your faith the greater the power of your being able for you to perform miracles will be. We can count on not having any more tears, no more defeats, or even forms of anguish, because He will over-rule all the inequities in your life. "We should rejoice in the Lord always" Philippians

4-4. We can find out that the miraculous power of the Holy Spirit starts out fresh each and every day; with the words of "Good morning Father God", thank you for the blessing you have given to me today and each and every day of my life. You need to let the power of the Holy Spirit rule in our hearts each and every day of our lives.

We all need to recognize that we don't have a button or a battery charger that we hook up to in order to refresh our bodies each day! We must depend on the words of Jesus and the power of the Holy Spirit to refresh our minds and our soul each and every day; God is in complete control. Don't ever get tired of saying Thank You God the Father Almighty for all you have given me.

In the Bible we can find many stories of the Miraculous Powers of the Spirit being used to get the message of God across to those God choose to receive it. God performed many and Jesus did too; but the Holy Spirit did them for both God and Jesus; all the Judges, Kings and prophets like Moses, Elijah, and Elisha. Elisha asked to be Elijah's servant and he at the time of Elijah's taking up to be with God; Elisha asked for a double portion of the Spirit is given to him. In 2 Kings we find that Elisha did perform twice as many miracles as that of Elijah.

Here are 7 areas to look at the Holy Spirit

1. His power is as it is with God and Jesus
2. He recognizes our needs.
3. He refreshes our minds every day.
4. He works on our inner hidden heart.
5. Helps us see visions of thoughts.
6. His healing Power is that of Jesus.
7. He has the power to increase your prayers

To me I look back at the creation for the greatest of the Miraculous Powers of the Holy Spirit. I see the use of the Holy Trinity working side by side just as inside of a triangle all of them working as one. God is the center of the power being given to the Father and to the Son and the Holy Spirit. God moved the Heavenly stars around to be what they are today, the Spirit moved the water to the firmament above exposing the land for man to live on and Jesus was asked to make mankind in their image, God said let mankind be made in our image.

We don't seem to see these kinds of miracles being done in this our world today! We do have some that we are told did happen. We do get testimony from those who have been prayed for through supplication that the people will be healed and those praying for the miraculous power to perform this supernatural thing with satisfaction. This is the same power that we want to use as that of the Day of Pentecost.

In the book of Job chapter 32; we find a friend of Job's telling us that he has a spirit with more power of knowledge and wisdom than any of Job's other friends. Elihu tells Job that his gift is being ignored by Job and his friends and that of God also. Many people can feel the power of the Spirit has come upon them; some can use the five senses of man. They are (Sight, Smell, Sound, Taste and Feeling.) In 1 Kings 19-11, "God said to Elijah to go outside and stand on the mountain; In the presence of the Lord, for the Lord is about to pass by." Elijah felt a powerful wind, like it was tearing the mountain apart, and shattering the rocks. That did not produce the vision of the Lord, and then he felt an earthquake, and didn't give Elijah a view of the Lord either. There was even a fire that came into view, but no Lord appearance either. Then in verse 12, a slight whisper came to his ears; he covered up his head and went outside to hear what the Lord had to say.

What is the difference between Healing and the Miraculous Power? We need to look back at the cross; where Jesus defeated Satan of his wicked ways. The power of the Holy Spirit comes from that power of Jesus and His teaching. Jesus paid the price for our sins at the cross. The promises of the cross will not be fully visible until His second coming. I'm talking about the lake of fire; where Satan will spend the rest of his days.

How many times have you heard the testimony of your fellow Christians, stating how they were healed? This to me is a miraculous discovery of what and how they have become healed! I feel that any and, all the Gifts of the Holy Spirit are quite miraculous. In the Book of Acts the 1st Century Disciples performed so many miracles that these too were considered to be miraculous.

In John 4-48; we see this, "Unless you people see signs and the wonders;" Jesus told them; "you will never believe." That's the way I see the world today; especially towards the last days. We can see in the book of Revelations (4: 1-12) even Gods two witnesses; could not get them to believe the end was nearer by (1260 days, or 42 months); they still didn't believe." They were to give prophecy during this time period; all that they were to preach of comes from the power of the Holy Spirit. They are to be given the power of fire coming down from the heavens; also power to shut up the heavens causing drought conditions. Then there is the power of turning the water into wine; and the plagues of all kinds. A beast will rise from the bowls of the earth and kill them but, in (3 1/2) three-half days they will rise up; given life from the breath of God. Gods command to them will be, "come up here". All of their enemies watched them rise up to God in heaven.

Surely this is an example of the Miraculous Powers of the Holy Spirit.

The more we see that the gifts of healing are taking place the better we can understand that these miracles are of the Holy Spirits Miraculous Power.

We pray for people every-day that must to go in for biopsies. When they get the results, low and behold they couldn't find anything there! Praise God for all He has done.

6

PROPHECY –

f. When I think of Prophecy I'm reminded that we as disciples are to spread the words that Jesus taught. Let us look at the facts of Jesus's mission here on earth! His mission was three (3) Fold, 1st Teach the 2nd to Proclaim and 3rd to Heal. His mission is carried out even today by you and me as Disciples of Christ Jesus. Jesus taught in Synagogues on the Sabbath, He taught to crowds proclaiming the Good News of God the Father and of Love for one another just as the Father wanted Him to do. Jesus was filled with the Holy Spirit of God on that day He walked into the River Jordan and was baptized by John. This same Spirit of God is available to you and I. Jesus healed everyone that asked of Him to do so. He even knew in advance of some that needed His hands on and Spiritual approach to healing. Jesus went into towns and taught and proclaimed and healed everyone before He left that town. The word spread from town to town, that Jesus was coming. God had to send His Son Jesus because the world was full of hate, sorrow, trouble and sin was crippling the whole nature of mankind; contrary to what God had planned for us. Man was lost in a Spiritual darkness; our eyes had to be opened up to see the beauty of what we could be when we loved one another.

Is there hope for the future; you had better believe there is. We are to prophesize the future of His second coming as in 1 Thessalonians 4: 16-18

"For the Lord Himself will come down from heaven with a loud command, with the voice of the archangel and the trumpet call of God, and the dead in Christ will rise first. After that we who are still alive and are left, will be caught up together with them in the clouds to meet the Lord in the air. And so we will be with the Lord forever. Therefore encourage one another with these words". This is one of the ultimate ways of how you and I can prophesize today; what can we teach, proclaim or even begin to understand how we can make someone see the future while living in present; remembering the words from the past as Jesus taught.

The New Testament use of Prophecy is a message for us to give to those who are in doubt, or lost in trying to figure out what direction they need to go in the word. Not everyone can become a prophet, but we need to recognize that when we receive a message we need to pass it on. In turn those who have a revelation that they can't figure out we need to be ready to explain it using the word of God! There are several areas we need to look at.

1. Recognize that all Gifts of the Spirit come from God.

2. Know that not everyone can become a prophet.

3. You must be filled with the desire to communicate in this gift.

4. Explain the value of Prophecy.

5. Explain the Authority of scripture.

6. Remember that this gift is not the only way to explain the power of the Spirit

7. Help others understand the questions and the answers are found in our hearts and the Holy Spirit will convict us as to the reasoning.

Remember this prophecy is God speaking to us through the Holy Spirit. It is different from the Old Testament; in the fact that God choose men to prophesize the future, today we get to explain the past, present, and the future. The greatest aspect of prophecy I think, is the foretelling of the future. We are to inform Gods people and those who need reassurance of those things about to come.

We should be reminded that the Great Commission of Jesus, (go forth and preach the word of the Gospel, get them to repent of their sins, baptize in the name of the Father and of the Son and the Holy Spirit.) Preach this unto the whole world.

It's ok if you want to act like the Old Testament's Samuel. He is a good example to follow.

You see Samuel listened and obeyed every word of God; He had the power of the Spirit.

In the Book of Revelations we get to look into the future of God's world! Do you remember the hearsay of the New Jerusalem; and its pearly gates where St. Peter will be greeting us when we get there? Well the picture I get is New Jerusalem will have twelve gates, the more the gates the more people can go and come ever so freely. So St. Peter is going to be real busy but the fact is the gates are there not to keep people from coming in but to give free access to God's Kingdom.

In Revelation 21-12; "The City of New Jerusalem had a great high wall with twelve gates and with twelve angels at the gates. On the gates were written the names of the twelve tribes of Israel." These gates were divided equally three on each side of the four directions of the compass. And the foundations had the twelve names of the Apostles.

Explaining the visions of St. John tells to us it is not an individual that will show up at the pearly gates but many will be coming in and out at the same time. In the early books of the Hebrew, we can find passages that tell us the world will be streaming in and out of the gates of the New Jerusalem because all those who God has set aside to believe in Christ Jesus; are invited to pursue the life that God had intended us to have back in the beginning of creation in the garden of Eden.

Prophecy of the visions of St. John should be an exciting experience; a breath taking one at that. The Tree of Life will be there the same one that God intended Adam and Eve to enjoy. The same tree that Eve eats the forbidden fruit from; was the one she was tricked by the evil-one. She then offered the fruit to Adam, and God called to them for their sin. I thank Father God, for giving to us His Son and for His dying for us on the cross; and taking away the sins of the world. As we give these visions of prophecies of the future; we want to give them in a light that will shed grace on our God for all He has done for us. God the Father has set standards for us and He wants us to know that He has always tried to engage us to a renewed love of Him and the life-giving ways He has set forth for us to follow. God is good.

7

SEEING SPIRITUAL GIFTS

g. God ultimately has one purpose; to save us from our sins. (Regardless if we think we have not sinned for all have sinned and come short of the Grace of God) The Bible states how this is possible in John 3:5 where Jesus said, "Except a man be born of water and of the Spirit, he cannot enter into the kingdom of God." Peter further clarified this in Acts 2:38 when he said, "Repent, and be baptized every one of you in the name of Our Lord Jesus, for the remission of sins, and ye shall receive the gift of the Holy Spirit." It is the receiving of the Spirit that causes us to be born of the Spirit. Since it was originally given during the celebration of Pentecost as recorded in Acts 2, those individuals who have been filled with the Holy Spirit, began their discipleships of preaching, teaching and healing those in need. Not only is the Holy Spirit essential for our salvation, He provides numerous benefits to our lives as well.

Jesus told His disciples they would "receive power when the Holy Spirit comes upon you" (Acts 1:8). The almighty God manifested in flesh as Jesus the Christ sent The Holy Spirit to His followers so they would have His power. The accomplishments of the Spirit filled Christians and their miracles were unsurpassed by any group in history. They healed the sick and lame, raised the dead, cast out demons and influenced people. It was said of them that they "have turned the world upside down" (Acts 17:6). These great acts have continued throughout history, from the days of the Christian persecution by the Roman

MY HOLY SPIRIT

Empire to the great revivals of the late nineteenth and early twentieth century's. It can be said that the most powerful person in the world is a Spirit filled Christian.

The stories in the Bible are true examples of how the power of God can work in our lives. Spirit filled Christians are not alone; they have the power of God behind them as they move through the world. Whether it is praying for a sick friend, enduring hard times, or simply teaching to someone about Jesus, the power of the Holy Spirit is always available.

The Holy Spirit also benefits us in other areas of our daily life. Galatians 5:22-23 likened this to a tree bearing fruit. "The fruit of the Spirit is love, joy, peace, patience, kindness, goodness, gentleness, faithfulness, and self-control". The Holy Spirit produces fruit in our lives. With the help of God's Spirit we can love other people in a super-natural way and treat them with gentleness, kindness, and goodness. With only our human ability we often treat others unkindly and fail to put them first; with the power of the Holy Spirit we can show true self-control and treat people right. With this supernatural love the first Christians were able to unify in such a way that the Bible says, "Nor was there anyone among them who lacked; for all who were possessors of lands or houses sold them, and brought the proceeds of the things that were sold, and laid them at the apostles' feet; and they distributed to each as anyone had need" (Acts 4).

From the Holy Spirit we can also receive during troubling times, joy and peace. By ourselves, we tend to give in and be controlled by our negative circumstances, but with the Holy Spirit, we can make it through any and all situations. In a raging storm we can have peace "which passes all understanding" (Philippians 4:7). When depression sets in, we can still have "joy unspeakable" (I Peter 1:8). When sick-ness takes hold or when the money runs low the Holy Spirit will give strength to carry on.

The Bible contains many examples of the benefits of being filled with the Holy Spirit, but it takes a personal experience to truly com-prehend these blessings. I wish I could explain in words of my own experience. But I can't, so let me tell you that my life since that day has been amazing. It hasn't been a walk in a beautiful rose garden; I have faced my share of trials, some of which I have failed very badly. But after each mistake, the Holy Spirit gave me the strength to get back up and continue on.

God will never give up on us. Let Gods peace sustain you; on the bad days His joy lifted my spirit. I have even shown love where I used to shown hate. And it was all because the Holy Spirit was working in my life. I don't deserve such a gift, but by the Grace of God through his Son Jesus He offered it to me anyway.

Hope is another blessing of the Holy Spirit. Paul says, "May the God of hope fill you with all joy and peace in believing, that you may abound in hope by the power of the Holy Spirit" (Romans 15:13). On a daily basis, the only thing that can get us through the day is hope. Jesus will return for those who have been born of the water and of the Spirit. Because of His Holy Spirit we have a hope beyond this world that one day we will see the kingdom of God where "there shall be no more death, nor sorrow, nor or crying. There will be no more pain" (Revelation 21:4). Pray until that day, that Glorious and Holy Day comes.

I believe I have said something in the understanding of the Holy Spirit is not found in receiving the Gifts of the Holy Spirit; but the real reason in becoming a Christian I feel is this, I would rather make use of the Fruits of the Spirit; we need to sow the seeds of the Fruits of the Spirit, that they may produce in each of us of how we can make them work so that we can serve our Lord and Savior, and use the Gifts of the Spirit in a loving and compassionate way.

Our overall actions in using the Fruits of the Spirit can cause us to see what the Spiritual Fruits can produce. Love is to follow the will of God, Joy is happy in what you share, Peace, setting examples of how we can act towards one another. Then there is the time to wait for results like as in our Patience. The example of being good, gentle, and showing kindness, is exercising our faithfulness to one another. Keeping it all together tells us we are in control; self-control that is. In all the Fruits are the inner workings of our outer examples of the Gifts of the Spirit. The Holy Spirit's works in us is through Grace and it is defiantly bound by our Faith, faith that can bring us enduring Hope; that we might be able to share the Glory of God, His Son and with the Power of the Holy Spirit.

CHAPTER 7   SUMMARY
OUR QUEST FOR BENEFITS

If we are to put our lives on a scale of one to a hundred; were to live for Christ; I would measure myself on the scale to be less than a ten (10 %). Living like Christ our Lord is not a natural thing for us to do. It is done in a supernatural way; we must yield to the Holy Spirit if we are ever to lead a life like our Lord and Savior Christ Jesus did! Let us look at Matthew 5: 43-48 "Love your neighbor; and hate your enemies." (This was a traditional thing in Jewish communities; it was also found in the writing of the Dead Sea Scrolls!

The Pharisees in the Old Testament interpreted; Love your neighbor as yourself; as to also mean; to also hate your enemies.) It was called the Rule of the Community! Jesus said; "I tell you to love your enemies and pray for those who persecute you."
God cause's the sun to rise and set on everyone in this world good people and bad people all at the same time. Christ tells us to be perfect, not that we can or ever will be but it is a standard that He sets for us to follow.

The Gifts of the Holy Spirit are a part of our personal (401K Plan). We are not to plan our retirement without His advice! Or you may end-up with the wrong kind of retirement plan and then you would have wasted the insurance policy that you had for your eternal home with God Almighty.

The seven gifts we discussed are our ways of grasping how we should live with one another, sharing not only the Gifts but exercising the Fruits of the Spirit also. Remember the Gifts of the Holy Spirit are the cake we need to eat and the Fruits of the Spirit are the icing on the cake.

We need to plan out our lives, in a way that we can be guaranteed a future without worries and where our future will home will be. Remember Job put his trust and faith in Gods Holy Spirit for his future, in spite of the pain and suffering he endured. He knew God would raise him from his trials, no matter how hard they were at the moment. Once we accept Jesus we have a secured spiritual future; and it has no expiration date. Why because Jesus died for us on the cross and rose again to save the lost. Our future is secure and is not ever, to be measured with doubt; His promises are true.

KNOWLEDGE:

a, From John 14-3; "When everything is ready, I will come and get you, so that you will always be with me where I am." With the knowledge of this passage, we need to be ready at all times.

Back in the early eighty's my wife and I were on a diving adventure, we flew from California in the good old U.S. of A; to Bali, Indonesia, with a stop off for refueling on the Island of Biak, which was some one thousand (1000) miles from Bali. We then flew after a few hours lay-over to Bali. We weren't prepared for this; as we didn't have sufficient knowledge of this part of the world! After a week of diving in the Bali area we then headed off to the Island of Sulawesi; to the city of Manado for ten more days of diving once again we lacked the knowledge of just where it was located. It was nine hundred miles north of Bali a few miles above the Equator. The plane ride was great; all the diving was outstanding and the diving experience of seeing the beautiful waters here in Indonesia have lasted us a life time; now here is a great awaking we faced.

We left there on a smaller plane they flew us back to Biak five hundred miles due east; when we arrived it was midnight and after one hour they closed the airport up and we were told to go outside and wait till it opened up again at five Am.

Wow we were all by ourselves no hotel or motel or benches, there wasn't anything. One of the worst feelings ever, is being stranded. We put our backs to the glass doors put our suitcase and equipment around us and Gloria lay in my lap and I stayed wide awake. How could this happen why didn't we have knowledge beforehand of this situation that lay before us. Oh did I tell you no one spoke English; all I knew was hello and good bye (Sala-mat-pa-gee) (tut-see). (This may not be correct either).

Thank God for John 14-3; that's one very good reason I believe that the second coming of our Lord Jesus is so reassuring to me. He will not leave me behind; He will keep His promise that He makes to all of us. He is preparing an eternal home for us like a Mansion on the Hilltop; He is going to guide us all the way to Our Fathers Home. Knowledge of the word of God can keep us informed; absolutely informed just read it and believe in His word.

WISDOM

b.   There was a Rabbi that said, "all the Commandments can be summed up into one; a call to love not only God but one another." In Mark 12: 29-31; we find Jesus saying this, "The most important Commandment is this; "Hear oh Israel: the Lord our God, the Lord is one. Love the Lord your God with all your heart and with all your soul, and with your entire mind and all your strength." "The second is this: Love your neighbor as yourself; there is no commandment greater than these."

In the Old Testament I found in Deuteronomy 6:4, there is a prayer called the (Shema) and till this day we find the Jews reciting this prayer of Jewish Faith every morning and evening in every Synagogue. "The Lord God is one and we should love Him and one another". As Jesus quoted the Verses in Mark 12: 29-31; so did the Jewish nation. They saw that their neighbors had too many gods and they were willing to share with their neighbors their God; as He is the one true God to love; and those who love Him He will protect; in Acts 10:35 we find this; God accepts from every nation who ever fears Him and is willing to do what is right. The wisdom I talk about here knows who God is and our need to please him.

I love looking up into the heavens I see all the beauty that God's Hands have created; but the real beauty is all around us. When we walk down the street we see His greatest achievement; that being mankind. Can you imagine the complexity of the human body and just how much wisdom would it take to create one better.

Our bodies are a proving ground for the Holy Spirit. He gives us whatever we ask for! I could never be a Doctor; the amount of knowledge to learn alone is mind boggling; never mind the wisdom to use all the information to care for the greatest of God's creation.

How much wisdom does it take to pick up a gun or a knife to kill someone? As I am writing this, it is twenty four hours after the massacre in San-Bernardino California. Sometimes people don't care what religion or race you belong to; it's the boldness of those who feel their religion or beliefs come first and try to force them on others is in plain truth against what God has in plan for all to accept Him and His Son .

My cat loves me for what I do for him; he seems to appreciate my feeding, petting and the attention I give him: how much wisdom does it take to show love for one another? God's law is summed up this way; Love God and your neighbor; as we pass this way in life but once, love is not a challenge it's a pure felling, which is known as love.

We have found that the seven benefits of the Spirit all come from God and His is the greatest of all Wisdom and He shares it with us thru His Son Jesus.

Jesus is the very essence of Gods Wisdom; and the Holy Spirit is the remembering source of Wisdom that we rely upon as He talks to our own spirit. We are blessed when we call upon the Spirit for assistance in all matters. He will lead us to a healthy and long life as we apply ourselves to Gods Wisdom. The Holy Spirit helps us preserve our lives, He protects us, and He helps us find joy, strength, and exalts us, so that we may be healed from life's ways and from any evils that might attack us. We must always call upon Him so that He can apply the Wisdom that we may need. There is a passage in Ephesians 1:7; "In Him (Jesus) we have redemption, through His blood, the forgiveness of sin, accordance with the riches of God's grace." We were slaves to sin and by His shedding of blood that washed away our sins we were set free; we are no longer held to the old laws of Moses Jesus is the Savior of the whole world; at least to those who accept Him as the Son of God.

Wisdom comes from Heaven, it is pure as the whiteness of snow, and it is a peace loving submission to the Holy Spirit. We can feel the fruits and the mercies of God; as we share what we have learned to others. In James 3:18; "We can be peacemakers who sow in peace, and reap a good harvest of righteousness."

FAITH

c.   When I looked at Faith I believed there might be two kinds. One how can we use faith in our daily lives; (like a wish come true or any daily chore we have to do are going to happen correctly). Then there is the trust we put in God's holy word along with the testimony of Jesus and His Apostles and Disciples; (like His Covenant to us). We are to believe that a wish or promises kept, is a Faith blessing given to us. We have to trust in something or someone and that it has come from a reliable source. We also have enough faith that whatever God gives to us means this; He gives it to us because He will keep all His promises.

There is the Faith of believing associated with our daily lives, when I take my key out and stick it in a lock it will open my house door, the engine of my car will start. Or the fact when I'm thirsty I turn on the faucet and the water comes out for me to drink. Then there are those things like a light switch which turns on or off, or my computer, when I finish typing and I hit save it will be there the next day. All that we do to function in our daily lives means we can go forward doing what we need to do to accomplish a useful or serving life for ourselves and others and their needs. The use of the Holy Spirits benefits of a believing Faith; are all around us.

In Chapter Three I talked about the subject matter, (Power of Faith) that comes from God; for what He says is the truth and He has revealed it to us in His Holy Word. I gave three examples of the (doubting Thomas syndrome). We live by faith and not by sight; how many ways does it have to be presented for you to believe; and how are we to respond to something we can't see?

We talked about the Power of Faith; what it means to us and how we saw it being used in the lives of people in the Bible; (Miriam, Moses, Jephthah, and Samson). Each of them was given task to do for the Lord. Each one did a fantastic job; but they managed to back slide; but with a request to the Holy Spirit they repented and prayed for their power and wisdom to return. The Holy Spirit did come upon each of them and He gave them each the Spiritual power needed to accomplish their task that they prayed for.

We do walk by Faith when we listen to what the Holy Spirit of God leads us to believe in our walk in life. He talks to us saying, without faith it is impossible to please God, and for those who use the Holy Spirit actually believe that He is God; and God rewards those that diligently seek Him, (Hebrews 11-6).

It is for the Glory of God that we all should accomplish the wonderful works that are assigned to us; no matter what we feel about them, do His bidding and His love will endure with us forever.

d.   What do Healing, Patience and Suffering have in common! First of all, we most certainly will be healed by our faith in our believing that Jesus through the Holy Spirit will be our answer! We must show our patients especially when it comes to healing our ailing bodies; in order for us to use them to their fullest of potentials; especially for the age we are; including our hearts and minds.

In James Chapter five we can find four aspects to a healing process; for instance we must not fight the Holy Spirit, or resist, nor resent or even seek retaliation for the ways we have gotten our bodies into, including our hearts and mind; it's a like a pain and suffering mode. We must look forward to a time that healing will take place. Doctors tell us this especially after surgery. He says after three days of rest start exercising, just enough to loosen up, then for two to three weeks increase your pace gradually; and then make an appointment with me in my office and we will then re-evaluate your progress before you get back to work!

The Holy Spirit looks after us as we give to Him our full attention through the power of our faith and of answered prayers.

I would like to talk about James of the Book of James; he is most likely the brother of our Lord Jesus. He was the one who did not believe that Jesus was the Son of God; or that He was the Messiah that the Jews were expecting. He did not believe until after Jesus was resurrected. James most likely was with His mother Mary when Jesus died on the cross. His witness the pain and suffering of Jesus and right along with his mother Mary they also felt the pain and anguish of Jesus dying on the cross. When Jesus arose from the Dead on the third day He spent forty days on earth and I personally believe and it's possible that Jesus may have spent time with James, James must have suffered in pain for his actions of not believing before; this would account for the changes in James you see, he had a complete turn-around he then believed that his brother Jesus was the Messiah and James became a very important Apostle for Jesus. He was the head of the Council at the Church of Jerusalem. He was involved in all the Church matters, he wrote letters of encouragement to all of the 12 Tribes; explaining what was going on, as the New Way of the Christians went forward. Remember this that any form of healing is a blessing from God Almighty; and it is to enhance the Church of God as it goes forward just as James found out.

Remember Job to had suffered, he never gave up on his love of God, nor did he resist all the pain and suffering. He had patience and did not fight back or resent what was happening to him. Job feed off the Spirit of God each and every moment of his life. He listened to Gods Holy Spirit and he testified to the pure love of God by his believing that his faith would carry him through all that was happening to him. Remember this that the Holy Spirit is within us all, and all we have to do is call upon Him; you should not have any doubts for He will be with us throughout all our pain and suffering and He will heal us.

e.   The Holy Spirit is the provider of all our Miraculous Powers. In 1 Corinthians 10; we find this the miraculous powers can be associated with the power of our deeds or the works we do.

What is the difference between Healing and miraculous powers? When we look back at the Cross; where Jesus defeated Satan because of his wicked ways of insisting we sin so we can get what we want in life.

The power of the Spirit comes from Jesus and what He has taught to each of us; it is because Jesus paid the price for our sins, past, present and future sins not only for you and me but for the whole world; especially those who accept Him as the Son of God. We must realize this, that the promises of the cross will not be fully realized until His 2nd coming. There is to be a lake of fire that Satan will be cast into; where he will spend the rest of all his days.

When Jesus went to His home town of Nazareth, He found not only the people of the town didn't believe in Him, i.e. Matthew 13 53-58; "who is this man, isn't He the Son of Joseph and His Mother is Mary; aren't those His Brothers; James, Joseph, Simon and Judas; and aren't those His sister over there." It would appear that only His mother Mary believed in Him; His earthly father most likely had passed on at this time. No one else believed, then in v. (58), "and so He did only a few Miraculous deeds there, because of their unbelief."

There are a couple of sayings we may want to look at! One is, "the beauty of things is in the eye of the beholder"; the other is "God works in mysterious ways"!

God's power of events or deeds of His works are done through the Holy Spirit. We get to visualize these events and/or experience them first hand when they occur and we then associate them as evidence of His powers of miraculous things happening right before our eyes.

God works in mysterious ways can also be said in this was; God performs miraculously in a mysterious way. When we use the words of works and deeds and Miraculous Powers; they could be considered as plural for what we need in explaining the use of the benefit of the miraculous power of the Holy Spirit.

What constitutes miracles; do we have any happening in this day and age? Did all the miracles occur with the Apostles in the 1st Century? I hear testimony every week of deeds and works that are found in the hearts of believers that something of a miracle has occurred in their lives. Christians confess that by praying or having others pray by supplication for them that they get healed or they receive something that is need to make their lives complete has come true. Many people fell the power of the Spirit has come upon them and they therefore receive an answer from either their friends or those of a Pastor or Ministers hands that were laid upon them. A healing has taken place and therefore the Miraculous Power of the Holy Spirit has been achieved.

f.   Prophesying should be our path that will lead us to sharing the word of the Gospel unto the whole world. As Christians of this age we are responsible to share the Prophecy of the 2nd coming of our Lord Christ Jesus! He will return; we have never been closer to this returning of Jesus than we ever have before. Our world is about to experience the most climatic event ever to be held! (Watch of the signs)

Each of us has the ability in prophesying this 2nd coming; we are to speak with all our strength, encourage and comfort one another. (1 Corinthians 14:3).

This is a gift of the Holy Spirit, we started out saying this; "the answer my friend's may be in the blowing of the wind".

When I look back to the Old Testament I see this, God often spoke to the Prophets when they were alone; His Spirit filled them with what to say and do. I personally have felt the Spirit guide me in what to say and do as I have prepared for a sermon or for teaching a class of the Bible; and yes writing this book on the Holy Spirit.

If I were to explain it in simple terms it would be like; (he touched me, He then made me like liquid, He then molded me, and I then experienced words I should say in order to enlighten all who have ears that they should listen. Let's look at 2 Peter 1: 16-21. Peter starts out with the experience at the Day of Transfiguration, He remarks that Jesus is in charge and that God is present and makes His presence known by saying "this is my Son whom I love, with Him I am well pleased". Present with them, in plain sight were Moses and Elijah; all of this is occurring through the power of the Holy Spirit. Can you see what I see here, that the presence of the Holy Trinity is made known to us! We have now become eye witnesses and can use this to make Prophecy known to all who are willing to listen. Peter also states that we have a prophetic message here something we can rely on and should pay attention to it. Also (V-20) "Above all you must understand that no prophecy or scripture came about by the prophet's own interpretation of things".

(V-21), we see this "Prophecy never had its begging in the will of Human kind; "but prophets through a human spoke from God's words as they were carried along by the Holy Spirit".

Make yourself familiar with those things in the Bible that need passing on, use the Holy Spirit to assist you in all matters; we realize He can't be seen or heard but when we listen to what our Hearts are telling us and what we fell can actually be seen as long as we believe, for it is by our Faith that we believe always, that all things are possible with God (Luke 1-37). And remember this; Let the Peace of Christ rule in our hearts always (1 Colossians 3-15). We should rejoice in the Spirit of the Lord always; (Philippians 4-4). God is the source of all scripture, so what it says to you is what God says; and you can believe that all His words are true.

g. We live in an era that seeing the results of our Spiritual Gifts is a blessing for each of us who believe in the Gospel. The 1st Century Apostles received the 1st Gifts of the Holy Spirit just as Christ Jesus said they would. They also used the Fruits of the Spirit to spread the Good News of the New Way in Worshiping God with Christ in us. We as Christians have a responsibility to share what we feel and what we can project for others to see.

Jesus told His disciples to go to the upper room and wait there until the gift of the Father (the Holy Spirit of God), to come upon them.

Do you remember the scale I introduced (1 to 100) Can you see a difference now as to your understanding before you had been informed about this version of Understanding the Holy Spirit! Have you seen your percentage increase; I pray that I have made a difference and have shed some new light on the Holy Spirit! This Chapter Seven is to be your 401K in your Quest for a stabilized Benefits program.

This would include a path that leads you follow Christ Jesus each and

Every day. Is your program filled with the gifts of the Spirit; like using the knowledge of what you learned with wisdom to share with faith! When you pray for someone to be healed do you feel comfortable in the fact that your plan gives a clear site of a miracle taking place! Are you able to go forth and prophecy the results of all these Spiritual gifts; that you have gained knowing the Holy Spirit has guided you on your quest? Any quest for a solid 401 K plan using the gifts and the fruits of the Holy Spirit will result in your ability of being a Christian in good standing. This means that you must set in motion a plan that is easy for you to see and understand. You must be very careful you do not seek help outside of the Word of God.

You must be able to distinguish between all the spiritual things that come to mind. In 1 Corinthians 12-10 tells us you have been given this gift to be able to see false prophecies that come from evil spirits.

In the Book of Revelation 2-7; we find that Jesus is speaking to the seven churches; He always says this, "Whoever has ears let them hear, what the Spirit says to the churches. To the one that is victorious, I will give the right to eat from the tree of life." Each letter challenges each church to be victorious against the battle of evil.

We need to keep our eyes upon those we are responsible for and ensure them that they are the children of God. In Habakkuk 1-12, we find this; "Gods eyes are to pure to look upon evil; He cannot tolerate wrong doing. Let us turn our eyes away from evil, just as God will not look at evil neither should we tolerate looking at unclean spiritual gifts. Evil flourishes right alongside of goodness, when it rains in rains on both the good and the evil ones.

FINAL COMMENTS

I would like to give you a final comment; especially on the speaking and interpreting of Tongue's. I looked at them as Paul and Peter did. (Using Romans 3:13, 14:11; Plus 1 Corinthians, 14: 1-25) I would suggest that everyone should read this verse's and become familiar with Tongues then, and today. These two gifts were used by the 1st Century Apostles; it appeared that they were trying to make them a common gift that would manifest within the Church; but they needed to be interpreted, and someone had to make sense of what was being said.

Now in the Book of Acts 10:44-46. It was the day of Pentecost and Peter was able to speak to all who were present inside and outside of the Upper Room. Peter spoke to all of them using one language even to the Gentiles. It was the Holy Spirit that came upon all of them; (V) 46, "For they heard them (the Apostles) speaking in Tongues all praising God". It appears to be an experience that is controlled by the Holy Spirit; because this gift does not imply any knowledge of a language by the one that was speaking of what was said or the receiving of the message. This most likely was coming from the Holy Spirit; and the interpretation is in believing that it came from God working in them rather than from any knowledge of a language.

So the one that is speaking and the one who is interpreting; has great Faith that God is speaking to him and he may only understand just a few words; but then the Holy Spirit gives each of them what they need in order to understand all of the translations. (V) 1, "Let love be your greatest aim; nevertheless, ask also for the special abilities the Holy Spirit gives, and especially the gift of prophecy, that being able to preach the message of God." To me this means that even thou Tongues are a specialty to converse with God; not everyone can do this, so preaching, evangelizing and teaching the word of God would be more advantages in reaching new converts.

Paul says in (V) 6, "Dear friends, even if I myself should come to you talking in some languages you don't understand how that would help you? But if I speak plainly what God has revealed to me, and tell you the things I know, and what is going to happen, and the great truths of God's word that being, what you need; and that is what will help you.

COME LET ME GIVE YOU THE HOLY SPIRIT

MY HOLY SPIRIT

COME FOLLOW ME TO THE HOLY SPIRIT

Lightning Source UK Ltd.
Milton Keynes UK
UKHW020651131119
353452UK00013B/1512/P